WHAT OT

"When it comes to coppers who could walk-the-walk and talk-the-talk there are none better than Steve Spingola. Guts, brains and savoir faire, Steve had it all. Now he has turned his considerable talents to giving readers real insight into the world of crime and detection, along with his perceptive commentary about privacy and liberty. You will truly enjoy the ride along with this remarkable lawman."
— *(Ret.) Captain Mike Massa, Milwaukee Police Department*

"Retired homicide detective Steven Spingola is a rare breed and truly an investigator to his core. Not satisfied with accepting anything at face value, he is examining the controversy at what must be a very uncomfortable intersection for anyone involved in law enforcement: liberty vs. technology. Spingola has dared to do what precious few of our best cops will and that is to take a long, hard look at the new technologies being used by law enforcement and how these technologies might adversely impact the freedoms of innocent Americans. As a good government and privacy advocate, I applaud Steve Spingola's courage in initiating this desperately needed debate amongst his peers and the public."
— *Kaye Beach, Norman, Oklahoma*

"Best of the Spingola Files, Vols. I and II peeks into the world of a veteran homicide detective: the complexities of victimology, the misnomer of a 'cold case,' and the quandary of constitutional preservation and technology. Steven Spingola's ego-free compilation begins by gently providing detail necessary to impart the brutality of certain unsolved cases while avoiding victim exploitation. Spingola weaves in a tease of the Milwaukee and Madison underworlds then stimulates critical thinking on the national policy of domestic surveillance, leaving one to long for the investigative journalism of yore."
— *Kelly McAndrews, J.D.*

"Steve Spingola earned the respect of his peers and supervisors during his tenure with the Milwaukee Police Department through hard work and positive results. I was impressed with his ability to relate to and teach young officers and detectives, which continues to this day through his Spingola Files montage, as well as his second career as a college-level police science instructor. Steve epitomizes the ideal of a police supervisor through his willingness to share his experiences in order to develop the talents of other law enforcement officers."
— *(Ret.) Captain Glenn D. Frankovis, Milwaukee Police Department*

BEST *of the* Spingola Files

Volumes I & II
(Print Edition Only)

Where the "sleuth with the proof" takes a fresh look at cold-case homicides and discusses issues of criminal justice import

Badger Wordsmith, LLC
Eau Claire, WI

STEVEN SPINGOLA

BEST OF THE SPINGOLA FILES, VOLUMES 1 & 2.

Copyright © 2012-2013 by Badger Wordsmith, LLC. All Rights reserved.

No part of this material may be used or reproduced in any manner whatsoever without written permission except in the case of brief quotations embodied in critical articles and reviews. For information: Badger Wordsmith, LLC, 2809 E. Hamilton Ave. #191, Eau Claire, WI, 54701, info@badgerwordsmith.com.

The author has done his best to present accurate and relevant information in this book. This book is sold with the understanding that the publisher and author are not engaged in rendering legal services or any other professional advice. In instances where opinions and/or speculation are provided, these views and opinions, unless attributed, are solely those of Steven Spingola

ISBN:	978-0-9796839-9-2
Author:	Steven Spingola
Forward:	Rick Sandoval
Copy Editor:	Livia Grogan
Comments by:	Mike Massa
	Kaye Beach
	Kelly McAndrews
	Glenn Frankovis
	Eric Donaldson

BEST OF THE SPINGOLA FILES, VOLUMES I & II (Print Edition Only)
Steven Spingola

Crimes and offenses—United States—Non-Fiction
Organized crime and offenses—Untied States—Non-Fiction.
Book Review—United States—Non-Fiction
Book Review—Milwaukee, Wisconsin, United States—Fiction
Government Surveillance—United States, Non-Fiction

Published by Badger Wordsmith, LLC
www.badgerwordsmith.com

FORWARD

As a young Milwaukee Police Department (MPD) street officer in the mid-1980s, I often sought the advice of crème de la crème senior personnel—those that stood head-and-shoulders above the rest; savvy coppers whose repertoires fused intelligence, integrity, an impressive work ethic, and a survivor's mentality. At the top of this list was Steve Spingola, an officer that I watched, and, ultimately, had the privilege to serve alongside of. I was impressed with his focus, his drive, and his seemingly endless supply of energy.

In neighborhoods riddled with street toughs, gangs, and gun fire, Spingola was a cop's cop, a person I, along with others comprising the thin blue line, could count on his bat-out-of-hell-type back-up. As an officer and detective, Steve's peers often deferred to his knowledge and expertise for answers to complex legal and procedural questions.

In the decades that followed, I watched as Spingola's stature grew exponentially throughout the halls of the MPD—first, as an extremely active street officer at District Five, where his name populated the merit arrest board; then as a renowned homicide detective, and, ultimately, as a lieutenant of detectives, where he supervised investigators in the violent crimes division of the Criminal Investigation Bureau and, later, the homicide unit.

Now, as a criminal justice instructor, fraud investigator, part-time detective, author, and investigative blogger, Steve Spingola continues to excel in the "normal" world. As an avid reader of the Spingola Files (SF), I can testify, first hand, that each month brings accurate, information-packed reading, such as a look at DNA science, a murder for hire scheme, and the use of drones for surveillance purposes.

The release of the Best of the Spingola Files, Volumes I & II to print promises to be a great catch for those who enjoy staying informed of the latest and hottest topics affecting law enforcement, privacy, and important issues before the courts.

— Rick Sandoval, Milwaukee Police Department (retired)

AUTHOR'S NOTE

Forensics, a Latin term meaning applied to law, enables victims to speak, figuratively, from the grave. To the untrained, casual observer, a contorted and/or mutilated dead human body is a morbid reminder that evil exists in the world. To a homicide investigator, human remains provide critical details concerning an individual's final moments on earth.

About four hours after death, post mortem lividity, caused by the accumulation of deoxygenated blood, begins to develop, as fluids move to the lowest point of gravity. Lividity observed in an area outside a body's lowest point of gravity, as well as the amount of blood found at a scene, is a telltale sign that the deceased was moved.

The death investigation of a former White House legal counsel, Vincent Foster, is a prime example of the importance of forensic science. In his book, The Strange Death of Vincent Foster, journalist Christopher Ruddy does an excellent job detailing the lack of blood evidence at the scene. The National Park Service Police put forth a theory that Foster committed suicide in small national park just miles from the District of Columbia, even though the amount of blood associated with a gunshot wound to Mr. Foster's head was noticeably absent.

In one of the Colonial Parkway murders, a killer almost decapitated Cathy Thomas while viciously slitting the 27-year-old woman's throat. During an epic struggle for her life, Ms. Thomas grabbed a few strands of the killer's hair, which investigators later found tucked between her fingers. Knowing that she might meet her demise, the struggling victim grasped for a an important piece of physical evidence that could lead detectives to the perpetrator. The killer(s) then stuffed the bodies of Cathy Thomas and Rebecca Dowski inside a compact vehicle, sent the car into a small ravine, and attempted to ignite the compartment with diesel fuel. The lack of significant blood evidence inside of Thomas' Honda is proof that these murders occurred elsewhere.

Unfortunately, father time, failed memories, ineptitude, and poor evidence collection methods, sometimes result in victims' cries from the grave going unheard; hence, the conundrum—too many killers remain at-large to murder again.

During the fall semester of 2009, a handful of students in a class I taught thought it odd that several organizations, such as the Innocence Project, diligently seek to exonerate those with alleged wrongful convictions, while few, if any, private groups advocate for the victims of unsolved homicides. In response, I started a blog, From the Notebook of a Homicide Detective, which later evolved into the Spingola Files (SF).

For the lack of a better term, my staff and I assumed the roles of investigative journalists, combing through online death investigation profiles, contacting sources, and searching newspaper microfilm. In most instances, SF chose to spotlight decades-old cases. Why? Over the course of time, the human condition changes. Spouses divorce or die; lovers are spurned; some find God and seek absolution; others decide it is time to come forward with a morsel of detail that might bring closure.

At SF, we are hopeful that the cases that my staff and I have chosen to profile might jar some memories. It is important to remember that, no matter how much time has expired, a statute of limitations for homicide does not exist. In death investigations, justice, although sometimes elusive, remains a persistent pursuit.

—Steven Spingola, Wales, WI

CONTENTS

The Face of Milwaukee Cold Cases 13
Detectives in the Rye: Part I 15
Detectives in the Rye: Part II. 17
Detectives in the Rye: Part III. 20
Detectives in the Rye: Part IV. 22
Killers & Campus. 25
Vanished but Not Forgotten 28
Wise Men let Dead Wise Guys Lie 31
Black and White Cloud of Retaliation: Part I. 33
Black and White Cloud of Retaliation: Part II. 35
Black and White Cloud of Retaliation: Part III. 37
Black and White Cloud of Retaliation: Part IV. 39
To Death do Us Part? 41
Serial Killer in Plain Sight for All to See. 43
Max & the Mob 46
Did Dahmer do It?. 50
M.P.D. Blue — A Portrait of Police Work 52
The Mysterious Whereabouts of Ralph Leon Jackson 55
Bad Week to be British in Madison 57
When Justice is as Blind as its Witnesses 60
The Honeybee Shooter Case: Circumstance or Coincidence?. 63
Police Believe Actual "Honeybee Shooter" is 10-7 65
This Holiday Season, Rats Needed 67
A Punishing Story of Rumor and Innuendo 69
Farwell Avenue Fait Accompli 71
The Mitchell Nevin Enigma 74
When Big Brother Reaches Out and Touches. 76
Beating Back the 'Bush'. 79

Deadpan Drifter	81
Prowlers on the Parkway: SF's Take on the Colonial Parkway Murders	84
Psychology of Homicide Presentation Now Available Nationally	88
Decades-Old Cold Cases Focus on Improved DNA Testing	89
Was Communication in Serial Stabbing Case Lacking?	91
The Falls Guy: Part I	93
The Falls Guy: Part II	95
A Cry from the Grave	97
Freedom Didn't Come Cheap for Former Saukville Copper	101
The Delaware Dumpster Debacle	104
Collateral Damage: Homicide Suspect's Son Gets a Pink Slip	106
The Fog of Time & Grafton Crimes	110
The Killer Conundrum	113
Leaving for College? Take Some Common Sense Along, too	116
Investigators Watch as Supreme Court Takes-Up GPS Case	119
Speakers Available to Discuss Milwaukee-Based Crime Novel	121
Shooting at the OK(auchee) Corral Still Under Review	122
Predator Spy Drones: Hovering Above your Town Soon?	125
Constitution 1, Big Brother 0–Top of the Second	127
SF Reviews "American Stasi: Fusion Centers and Domestic Spying."	128
When the Shoe is on the Other Foot, the Data Revolution Makes Those in Blue Cringe	131
SF Reader Alert: Be Aware of DNA Sharing	133
Conviction in Phoenix Bombing Connects the Loose-Ends	135
One Woman's Willingness to Stand-Up to Orwellian ID Act	138
Old School Sleuths Weigh-In on Most Current Crop of Detectives	140
Liberty Activists Doing the Job the Media Used to Do	143
Security vs. Privacy: an Interview with WUWM	146
The New 'Mark of the Beast' has Investigators Lovin' It	147
Lapdogs: the Media and the Surveillance State	149
Madison's Curmudgeon Mayor Seeks to End an Era He Created	151

Drones and the Judge 153
Majority Report: is the Electronic Iron Curtain Call upon Us?........... 155
Do-Gooder Signs Provide Solace for Active Shooters 157
Demands for Cell Phone Records Show Big Brother is Watching......... 159
NYC's Mayor and the Big Apple Police State 161
Feds Seize Former Marine, Eagle Scout for Facebook Posts 163
Update: Circuit Court Orders Brandon Raub's Release.................. 165
Is the U.S. Department of Justice
Targeting the Views of Military Veterans?.............................. 166
Police Chief's Association Lobbies
Against Anti-Big Brother Legislation 168
Why NSA is an Acronym for 'Never Say Anything' 171
Drew Peterson Case: Will the Guilty Verdict Stand?.................... 172
U.S. Rep. Jim Sensenbrenner Supports Landmark Privacy Bill........... 176
Ask the Cop on the Beat: Joe Biden Knows Better 177
Police Blotter: Gangsters, Shootings, and Defective Chinese Products.... 180
The Library Detective 182

THE FACE OF MILWAUKEE COLD CASES

NOVEMBER 10, 2009 | FILED UNDER HOMICIDE

Mention the name Nancy Radbil to a life-long Milwaukee resident over 45 years-of-age and they will likely recall the tragic death of an attractive young woman with thick, dark hair whose life likely ended near a northwest side bike path. Nancy, just 19-years-of-age, was last seen alive on the afternoon of July 2, 1979, while riding her bicycle along the north Menomonee River Parkway. Her parents later summoned the police when she failed to return to the family's home near N. 66th Street and W. Capitol Avenue.

After interviewing family members and neighbors, investigators believed Nancy was a missing and endangered person. Law enforcement officers and citizen volunteers extensively searched the area surrounding the parkway. Almost three days passed before investigators caught their first break. At about 1:30 PM on July 5, a methodical search by two officers paid-off. After removing a 150-pound manhole cover in the 5400 block of N. 111th Street, the officers discovered Radbil's clothes at the bottom of the sewer basin. Milwaukee police and volunteers then focused their attention to the area of the bike path just a block to the east.

On July 6, Richard Radbil, the missing woman's 26-year-old brother, and another volunteer, discovered Nancy's body about 120 feet east of the paved bike path in the 5500 block on N. 111th Street.

"Oh my God, my God, I found her," shouted a volunteer. Under her corpse, detectives discovered a shoelace and the woman's undergarments. The perpetrator had slashed Nancy's throat, causing a six-and-half inch laceration. At the scene, Richard Goeb, a specialist from the Milwaukee County Medical Examiner's office, told the Milwaukee Sentinel that the body "had been there several days." An autopsy later concluded that Nancy Radbil was also a sexual assault victim. "It's a cold one for now," an unnamed police captain told the Milwaukee Sentinel. "I wish we could have found her. You're out here looking for her, but you hope...[for] something else than what you know it is." Milwaukee police conducted an extensive canvass of the area surrounding the north Menomonee River Parkway. Two teenagers told investigators that they observed a Honda motorcycle with a red gas tank in the bushes of the parkway near 5500 N. 111th Street earlier in the week. Initially, the boys thought about stealing the seemingly abandoned motorcycle but had second thoughts. "Several persons have told police Tuesday," said an article in the July 10, 1979, Milwaukee Sentinel, "that they observed a man parked on a motorcycle near the spot where Nancy Lynn Radbil's body was found along the little Menomonee River Parkway." Investigators poured over records from the Wisconsin Department of Transportation in search of owners of this particular Honda motorcycle, but were unable to develop a solid suspect. According to witnesses, the well-traveled bike path near the crime scene was safe during the daylight hours. Detectives theorized that, having stopping for a rest along the bike path, the killer ordered Radbil into a secluded area at knifepoint, where he sexually assaulted and then murdered the young woman. The discovery of the victim's clothing at the bottom of the sewer secured by a 150-pound manhole cover suggested that the suspect possessed above average strength. Just five days prior to Nancy Radbil's disappearance, another woman was attacked near the Menomonee River Parkway. According to the Milwaukee Sentinel, "A man tried to pull the woman from her car while she was parked at 10433 W. Appleton Avenue," about a half a mile northeast of the Radbil crime scene. "She escaped, and the man then drove away in her car, which was later found burned." The Radbil case file contains interviews of dozens of persons, including convicted sex offenders. In one instance, detectives flew to Europe to speak with a US Army enlisted man who lived in the neighborhood where searchers found Radbil's body. While stationed in Germany, some investigators believed that the soldier attempted to strangle prostitutes. Today, Nancy Radbil's brutal murder remains one of Milwaukee's highest profile cold cases. The killer, if he is still alive, is likely in his early to mid-sixties. Individuals committing sexual homicides typically act to fulfill their demented sexual fantasies. Rarely, do they only take just one life, which is why it is important to keep the murder of Nancy Radbil in the public eye.

DETECTIVES IN THE RYE: PART I

NOVEMBER 22, 2009 | FILED UNDER HOMICIDE

"At any given time," I explained during a September 8, 2009, interview with WTMJ AM620 talk-show host Jeff Wagner, "there are between 25 to 50 serial killers active in the United States."

But investigations get increasingly complex when homicides committed in close proximity share similar methods of operation. When drug addicts, prostitutes, and psychopaths co-mingle, the details surrounding an individual's final moments on Earth are often times murky. After all, it is possible for one particular locale to have more than one serial killer active at a time, even if it drives detectives crazy.

The slaying of Ophelia Preston raises an important question: was more than one serial killer active in Milwaukee between 1986 and 2007?

On October 22, 1994, a man collecting aluminum cans discovered Preston's body in the rear of 1746 N. Martin Luther King Drive. The killer placed the known prostitute headfirst into a garbage cart. During the early to mid-1990s, prior to the re-gentrification of the Brewers Hill neighborhood, street-walking prostitutes frequented this area just north of Milwaukee's downtown.

Checking the serial numbers of the city-owned garbage cart, investigators ascertained that the trash receptacle did not belong to the King Drive address.

An autopsy revealed that Ophelia Preston died of manual strangulation. She had a telephone number in her pants pocket. A check of records linked this number to a City of Milwaukee employee, who, during the course of his duties, drove a yellow city truck and had access to garbage carts.

During his initial interview, the city employee denied having contact with Preston. When confronted with physical evidence, however, this man admitted he had met the victim at The Friendship Club, a community based facility Preston visited in an effort to kick her addition to crack cocaine.

Located in one of the toughest sections of Milwaukee, alcoholics and drug addicts frequented the area adjacent to The Friendship Club to give blood, and then trade the few dollars they received at the closest liquor store or drug house.

The city employee later admitted that he gave Preston a ride and had a "dope date" with the murder victim just three days prior to her body being discovered.

Having personally investigated this case, the proof needed to affect an arrest was growing.

NEXT: The detectives in the rye develop possible suspects.

DETECTIVES IN THE RYE: PART II

NOVEMBER 29, 2009 | FILED UNDER HOMICIDE

In late October 1994, officials from the Milwaukee Police Department believed that they had caught a break in the investigation of multiple strangulation homicides. The telephone number found in the pocket of Ophelia Preston led investigators to a City of Milwaukee employee who had access to a yellow city-owned truck and city-owned garbage carts.

A colleague and I stopped by the man's home in the 4900 block of N. Green Bay Avenue. After knocking at the front door, the city worker refused to answer. While we waited outside, the man telephoned his attorney and then the Milwaukee Police Department's Communications Division, explaining that he did not want contact with law enforcement. Although the city worker remained a suspect, investigators lacked a specific nexus connecting him to the Preston homicide.

About a year later, Milwaukee police arrested the same city employee after a woman claimed the man raped her. Police obtained a search warrant for the suspect's home that turned-up little. The city worker told police that he had a "dope date" with the woman. After reviewing the matter in its totality, the Milwaukee County District Attorney's office declined to issue criminal charges.

Since 1986, investigators had yet to clear eleven strangulation homicides of female drug users and/or prostitutes. In several of these cases, the killer(s) method of operation were somewhat similar, although the signatures slightly differed.

Things changed with the arrest of a north side handyman.

On November 21, 1997, police put the grabbis on George "Mule" Jones, 52, for the strangulation slaying of 24-year-old Shameika Carter.

Two days earlier, police discovered a woman's body behind a series of abandoned homes near N. 24th and W. Chambers Streets. Inside a garbage cart, under a pile of old, discarded clothing and clad only in a bra, was Carter, who had died of manual strangulation. Witnesses told police that Jones routinely worked on nearby abandon homes and resided just a few blocks from the crime scene.

A drug dealer later told investigators that Jones and Carter had stopped by his residence.

After leaving the dealer's flat, Jones and the woman parted company. Carter then purchased marijuana and returned to Jones' apartment.

While in the basement of Jones' home, Carter made sexual advances, removed her clothing, and shared a primo—a marijuana cigarette laced with crack cocaine. The rush caused Jones to experience an excruciating headache.

"George Jones stated that he did not plan on killing Shameika Carter," the criminal complaint read, "but when she laughed at him [about his lack of sexual arousal due to headache], he lost it" and strangled the woman.

Jones told investigators he blacked out, woke up the next day, and disposed of Carter's body.

Nicknamed the "mule" after his steady but awkward stride, Jones had a 1973 Mississippi manslaughter conviction for the sexually motivated slaying of a woman. After arriving in Wisconsin in 1979, Milwaukee police arrested Jones 17 times. In the ten months prior to the homicide of Shameika Carter, Jones had twice attacked other women.

In February 1997, after smoking marijuana with a woman half his age, the mule solicited a sexual act. "I love you," Jones told the woman, "and would go to jail for raping you." Jones then began to strangle the woman, ripped off her shirt, and punched her repeatedly before the woman fled through a bedroom window.

Two months prior to the Carter murder, while on probation for the February incident, neighbors witnessed Jones "beating an unidentified black female in the first floor bedroom." The neighbors intervened and separated Jones and the woman. However, since the woman fled before the police arrived, her identity remained a mystery.

Even though Police Chief Arthur Jones warned the media that the unsolved strangulation cases might be the handiwork of more than one killer, some reporters strongly suspected the mule was a serial killer.

On November 26, the Milwaukee Journal Sentinel ran the headline "2 women escaped attacks by suspect, police say." On November 28, the same newspaper printed a large graph depicting Jones' numerous arrests, an obvious attempt to link him to the unsolved strangulation homicides.

In a November 29 column, Milwaukee Journal Sentinel columnist Joyce Evans interviewed a prominent forensic psychiatrist. "If a serial murderer is stalking our streets," said George Palermo, "he would fit the profile of a non-social, lustful serial killer who thinks he's on a mission to cleanse the streets of prostitutes or drug addicts—women he probably despises."

The speculative reporters failed to note that Dr. Palermo's profile hardly fit the description of George "Mule" Jones.

NEXT: another suspect emerges.

DETECTIVES IN THE RYE: PART III

DECEMBER 5, 2009 | FILED UNDER HOMICIDE

After the November 19, 1997, arrest of George "Mule" Jones, some Milwaukee police officials expressed optimism that they had nabbed the man responsible for as many as 11 strangulation deaths of women involved in prostitution and drugs. Reading between the lines and taking their cue from sources within the Milwaukee Police Department, the media portrayed the mule as a probable suspect.

Yet the travels of those involved in the vice underground—prostitutes, drug addicts, and freaky sexual deviants—are difficult to establish. These individuals live on the fringes of society, where the major focus of their daily existence is fulfilling the urges brought about by substance abuse and sexual fantasies. The lifestyles of those involved make it difficult to develop a reliable investigative timeline.

Even when information presents itself that seems to shed some clarity on the goings-on of the vice underground, such as the arrest of George "Mule" Jones, other crimes often muddy the waters.

For example, on November 9, 1997, police discovered the body of Wanda Harris under a pile of tires in the 2000 block of W. Fond du lac Avenue, just two-and-a-half blocks east of The Friendship Club—a community based alcohol and drug treatment facility frequented by Ophelia Preston and another strangulation victim, Shelia Farrior. According to an autopsy report, Harris, a prostitute, died from strangulation.

On the same day that police officials made George "Mule" Jones' name public, detectives apprehended a 19-year-old Milwaukee man for the slaying of Harris.

"Authorities are checking the man's background," noted Milwaukee Journal Sentinel reporter Jessica McBride, "to see whether he might have been responsible for the other murders."

The suspect, Triru Dillie, later told detectives that he had paid Harris for sex, but killed the prostitute after she tried to rob him. A jury later convicted Dillie, who is currently serving a 131-year prison sentence.

In the fall of 1997, it appeared additional suspects were popping-up with each homicide. The lifestyles of victims and suspects tended to overlap, as each had similar backgrounds.

Investigators noted that George "Mule" Jones kicked-in to slaying of Sameika Carter, but denied killing others. Dillie's age—he was just eight-years-old in 1986 when the first strangulation murder occurred—caused investigators to rule him out as the serial killer.

Today, Dillie, now 38, is a part of a specially trained group of volunteers providing hospice care to dying fellow inmates in the Wisconsin prison system.

"You try to comfort them, as much as a person can," Dillie told the Wisconsin State Journal in March 2009. "We don't try to force anything on them. We find it is a privilege to be with them when they die."

Ironically, one can only wonder if Dillie shared the same appreciation for the life he snuffed out 11-years earlier.

DETECTIVES IN THE RYE: PART IV

DECEMBER 12, 2009 | FILED UNDER HOMICIDE

Over the course of a 23-year period, a possible serial killer, as well as a handful of other men from Milwaukee, murdered over a dozen women involved in prostitution and drugs. In late 1997, after the arrest of George 'Mule" Jones, the Milwaukee Police Department established a serial killer task force.

The task force did clear some homicides, but 11 slayings remained unsolved. On August 3, 1986, the body of 18-year-old Marie A. Smith was found floating in Northridge Lake on the far northwest side of Milwaukee. Cause of death: strangulation. On October 10, 1986, police discovered the body of Debra Harris, 31, at 144 N. Ember Lane on the near north side. Cause of death: strangulation. Just a day later, on October 11, 1986, investigators found Tanya Miller's corpse at 2123 N. 28th Street. Cause of death: strangulation. Police found the body of Irene Smith on November 28, 1992, near N. 7th and W. Burleigh Streets. Cause of death: strangulation. Smith also sustained stab wounds. On September 7, 1993, the body of Mary L. Harris was discovered stuffed in a garbage cart near N. 10th Street and W. Meinecke Avenue. Cause of death: strangulation. On October 13, 1994, Carron Kilpatrick's partially dismembered body turned-up inside a garbage cart near N. 6th and W. Burleigh Streets. Cause of death: strangulation. Kilpatrick also sustained stab wounds. The killer severed one of her legs, and sawed the other, but, for whatever reason, failed to finish the job.

The next two homicides were those I investigated. Florence McCormick (April 25, 1995) and Shelia Farrior (June 27, 1995) both died of ligature strangulation. The e-magazine expose I authored for Amazon.com, The Killer in Our Midst: the Case of Milwaukee's North Side Strangler, provides specific details pertaining to the McCormick and Farrior crime scenes. On August 30, 1995, two young boys using an abandoned mattress as a makeshift trampoline noticed that the springs failed to provide the usual amount of lift. The reason: a killer used the mattress to conceal the body of Jessica Payne, a 16-year-old runaway from suburban South Milwaukee. Cause of death: Payne's throat was violently slashed.

Twenty-two months later, on June 20, 1997, investigators located the body Joyce Mimms, 41, in a vacant home in the 2900 block of N. 5th Street. Cause of death: strangulation.

Almost ten years later, Ouithreaun Stokes, 28, was found dead in a vacant home at 3128 N. 7th Street. Cause of death: strangulation.

In prison at the time of the Stokes homicide, detectives scratched Jones and Dillie off their lists of serial suspects, even as the multiple strangulation homicides, many with similar but slightly different signatures, threw a wrench into the various theories of investigators.

From 1986 through September 2009, the Milwaukee Police Department had interviewed thousands of people regarding the strangulation murders of women in this high-risk victim group (i.e. prostitution and drugs). Each case, standing alone, had its own complexities; however, the matrix became increasingly complicated when grouped together.

Homicides of persons involved in the vice-underground are difficult to solve for a variety of reasons. In many of these investigations, it was difficult to find witnesses. Not many people are willing to step forward to provide information that may very well implicate them in criminal activity. Moreover, it appeared that the suspect premised his attacks on the absence of probable witnesses. Most serial killers tend to act alone and do not typically discuss their crimes with others.

Over time, however, DNA science would bridge the gap and speak from the victims' graves. Over the course of the last decade, advances in DNA testing have improved dramatically. Even though DNA technology, as we know it today, did not exist in the 1980s, in many instances the detectives and forensic investigators processing crime scenes properly recovered and packaged hundreds of pieces of evidence. As a result, forensic science currently uses contemporary technology to test evidence for crimes that occurred two or three decades previous.

And it was modern science, coupled with solid heels-to-the-pavement detective work, that resulted in the September 2009 arrest of Walter Ellis—the man charged with the homicides committed by the North Side Strangler.

Aware that DNA would implicate him in the strangulation deaths of several women, Ellis gamed-the-system when, eight years earlier, he convinced a fellow inmate to provide a sample for him. A search warrant executed at Ellis' residence in August 2009 ultimately resulted in the recovery of his legitimate DNA, which linked him to eight murder victims. Ellis pled guilty and is currently serving multiple life terms in prison.

The Detectives in the Rye—the title of this post—is an obvious play on one of the classic novels of all-time. In J.D. Salinger's The Catcher in the Rye, first person character Holden Caulfield shares a fantasy of himself as the caretaker of children playing in a large rye field that suddenly ends near a steep cliff. Caulfield saw it as his role to catch these children before they tumbled to their deaths.

While Salinger's character fantasized about catching the innocent, those investigating the slew of strangulation deaths sought to apprehend the nefarious trolling Milwaukee's rye field in search of new victims.

KILLERS & CAMPUS

DECEMBER 19, 2009 | FILED UNDER HOMICIDE

A rite of passage for high school graduates occasionally develops into a nightmare for a handful of parents. Their sons or daughters head-off to college; but, instead of earning a degree, they end-up a statistic—a victim of foul play.

Over the course of the last two years, crimes involving students from Wisconsin's two major state colleges — in Madison and Milwaukee — have made headlines. Many involve young women. Some remain unsolved.

In November, the UWM Post, a University of Wisconsin-Milwaukee student newspaper, weighed in with an editorial questioning Forbes Magazine's ranking of the city as the second safest in the country.

"Is this the same Milwaukee where students frequently receive campus safety alerts about robberies and assaults?" the editorial writer asks. "Is this the same city that is above the national average of violent crime rates?"

Milwaukee is a large city with dozens of neighborhoods with socio-economic and cultural differences. True, crime ravages some neighborhoods, although statistics indicate that others, such as the Upper East Side and downtown, are very safe. In these areas, crimes tend to occur when people lower their guards by traveling alone at night or leaving a local watering hole noticeably intoxicated. Nonetheless, comparing the crime rate near a college campus is similar to tallying the casualties of a small war—the numbers may seem minuscule unless, of course, the victim is someone you know and love.

To get a better idea of how UW-Milwaukee rates, consider the area on or near the UW-Madison campus. Madison is one-third Milwaukee's size. The city's politicians claim the state capitol is one of the safest cities in the Midwest, even though the homicides of ten women—killed on or near campus—remain unsolved.

Here is the list.

On April 2, 2008, 21-year-old Brittany Zimmermann's fiancé returned to their W. Doty Street apartment to find her stabbed and bludgeoned to death. The crime scene was so bloody he believed that Zimmermann, a senior at UW, died of gunshot wounds. Approximately 50 minutes earlier, in the midst of the fight for her life, Zimmermann dialed the Dane County 911. The call taker claimed that the young woman's voice gave no indications that she was in distress. Information, however, contained in a affidavit in support of a search warrant indicates that the recording of Zimmermann's call contains the sounds of a struggle. Investigators suspect an unidentified drug fiend looking for money killed the co-ed.

A young woman with a reputation for partying, Kelly Nolan went missing on June 23, 2007, during an evening of bar hopping. An employee of Amy's Café was with Nolan the night she disappeared near the State Street Brats tavern. Police located her decomposing body near Schneider Rd. in the Town of Dunn, about ten miles south of Madison.

UW-Madison student Julie Raasch made a fateful decision to hitchhike home to Merrill, Wisconsin on October 11, 1984. A friend observed the junior business major hitching about two miles from campus. He provided Raasch with a ride to Highway 54 in Portage County, where Raasch, some believe, attempted to hitch another ride. Deer hunters discovered her partially clad and badly decomposed body on November 17. Cause of death: probable strangulation.

On July 2, 1982, 19-year-old Donna Mraz made her way home from a job as waitress near Madison's trendy State Street area. Taking a short cut near Camp Randall Stadium, a man attacked and stabbed Mraz repeatedly. A witness heard the young woman's screams and arrived on scene just long enough to catch a glimpse of the killer.

Shirley Stewart was just 17 when she left her house-cleaning job on January 2, 1980. A group of students found her badly decomposed body in a state park just north of Madison. The probable cause of death: strangulation.

A 16-year-old hiker found the skeletal remains of Julie Speerschneider near the Yahara River almost two years after she was last seen alive in March 1979. Speerschneider had left the 602 Club, a tavern on University Avenue, and was last seen exiting a white compact car with an unidentifiable male companion near Johnson and Brearly Streets.

Twenty-four-year-old Susan LeMahieu disappeared on December 14, 1979. A group of bird watchers discovered her body in heavy brush about 50 yards from the UW Arboretum. An autopsy revealed she died of multiple stab wounds to the chest.

Julie Ann Hall was last seen celebrating her new job at Madison's Main King Tap, a few blocks east of the Capitol Square. Investigators found her remains in a shallow grave near Waunakee, just 12 miles north of Madison. She died of blunt force trauma to the head.

Debra Bennett left her apartment on Madison's north side evicted, barefoot, and broke. Police discovered her badly burned body in a ditch in the Town of Cross Plains on July 21, 1976. Oddly enough, three weeks after police discovered Bennett's body, an unknown party mailed her room key back to the Cardinal Hotel.

UW student Christine Rothschild left for her morning walk on May 26, 1968, and never returned. A student sneaking a peak into a Sterling Hall window found Rothschild's body in a cluster of thick bushes. The killer stabbed the 18-year-old freshman multiple times.

In several of these cases, investigators suspected John Lee Lucas and his sidekick, Otis O'Toole. The two traveled throughout the United States. Some investigators suspect that the drifters are responsible for hundreds of homicides. Former Dane County Sheriff Jerome Lacke was of the opinion that Lucas was responsible for the Speerscheider and Hall homicides. Since Lucas apparently fabricated several confessions, these cases remain officially unsolved.

While the editorial board of the UWM Post is right to be concerned about the rash of robberies of students near campus, the only homicides involving UW-Milwaukee students occur far from the university. One can only imagine the outrage if bird-watchers stumbled upon a decomposing student's body in Downer Woods, akin to the proximity of the LeMahieu homicide on the UW-Madison campus. Nonetheless, stranger homicides are difficult to solve no matter where they take place, which is why it is important to never walk alone at night, drink to excess, or walk away, unannounced, from a group of friends.

VANISHED BUT NOT FORGOTTEN

JANUARY 5, 2010 | FILED UNDER TRUE CRIME

"Never make a decision when you're mad," a veteran police officer long ago told me. "Nothing good will come of it."

Over the course of my career, I have worked hundreds of crime scenes brought about by unbridled anger, unchecked emotions, and fits of rage.

This was the case nearly 21-years ago when an attractive young women set out to confront the young man she had been seeing. Sandra Bertolas discovered that her supposed boyfriend had lied about his address, his last name, and conveniently forgot to mention a steady relationship with another woman.

On April 24, 1988, Sandra, just 20 at the time, told her friends that she was "going to have it out" with the man. At about 8:30 p.m., she left her parents' home in the Milwaukee suburb of Menomonee Falls.

Her family has not heard from her since.

Police located her locked car parked outside the Red Carpet Lanes in West Allis, approximately 12 miles from her home. Bertolas' two-timing boyfriend became an immediate person of interest, but claimed he never made it to the bowling alley. Investigators found no indication of foul play inside of the woman's vehicle.

An extensive search ensued. Police soon learned that the suspect's father was the caretaker of St. Adalbert's Cemetery, located on Milwaukee's south side. The suspect resided with his father in the caretaker's residence. Investigators scoured the cemetery's records for burials that occurred near the time Bertolas went missing. They even searched the grave of another woman to no avail. It appeared that Sandra Bertolas had simply fallen off the face of the earth.

But the presumed killer's cunning was met head-on by the tenacity of the missing woman's family and friends.

Sandra was the last of Albert and Dorothy Bertolas' eight children. The large, well-respected family, led by grade school educators, had built a reservoir of goodwill over the years. Those whose lives they touched seemed intent on repaying their gratitude in an effort to locate Sandra and bring the perpetrator to justice.

"I learned more from him [Albert Bertolas] in a huddle on the playground than from the other teachers in the classroom," a former Milwaukee police officer and private investigator Gerry Broderick, told Milwaukee Sentinel columnist Bill Janz.

Broderick agreed to work the case pro bono.

A psychic from Chicago and cadaver dog handlers also provided services free of charge.

The Bertolas family and their friends followed every lead and rumor. They searched farm fields, lakes and sewers, but found nothing. Ten years later, in December 1998, a tipster contacted the Menomonee Falls Police Department to report a bad odor emanating from the railroad tracks running through Jackson Park, about three miles north of St. Adalbert's Cemetery, near the time of Sandra's disappearance. Search dogs hit on a scent. Authorities then summoned cadaver dogs but, again, found nothing.

In the interim, the case took a strange twist. Sandra's brother, Alan Bertolas, soon learned that the man his sister was set to meet on that fateful night in 1988 applied to become a civil servant.

"A Milwaukee firefighter," noted the Milwaukee Journal Sentinel's Bill Janz in his May 1, 1998, column "is positive that his sister was murdered by a Milwaukee firefighter."

This did not sit well with many of those staffing the city's firehouses. Alan Bertolas contacted elected officials and higher-ups in the fire department, but, since investigators lacked evidence needed to support criminal charges, they could not intervene.

Once the purported suspect graduated from the fire academy, Janz reports that Alan Bertolas' friends on the fire department "made it as miserable as they could for the suspect." Fellow firefighters posted Sandra Bertolas' missing posters where the suspect worked. On another occasion, when the man stopped by a tavern with fellow firefighters, Gerry Broderick had the bartender page Sandra Bertolas, which "startled and unsettled the suspect."

Nonetheless, as time continued to slide by without a resolution, the investigation ran cold. Then, on April 24, 2001, 13 years to the day of Sandra's disappearance, Waukesha County District Attorney Paul Bucher initiated a John Doe probe.

In Wisconsin, a John Doe investigation is similar to a grand jury at the federal level. The hearings are secretive. Typically, the only players present are a judge, a prosecutor, a bailiff, and a stenographer. The court swears witnesses under oath and takes testimony seeking to unearth previously unknown details of a crime. If a witness chooses to exercise their Fifth Amendment right not to testify, a prosecutor may grant use immunity; whereby, the truthful information provided by a witness, as well as any fruits of that testimony, are immune from use in a criminal prosecution of the testifier. If a witness refuses to testify after an offer of immunity is given, the judge can jail the witness on a charge of contempt.

In this instance, the John Doe probe was unusual for one reason: the evidence seems to suggest that, if Ms. Bertolas was a victim of foul play, the crimes probably occurred in an adjacent jurisdiction—Milwaukee County. It appeared that since the Bertolas family resided in Waukesha County, their county's prosecutor was using his office's resources to give the family closure.

But after 13 months of examining over 50 witnesses, Waukesha County Circuit Court Judge J. Mac Davis determined that the hearings fell short of the sufficient evidence needed to file charges.

"We hope that this would end this finally for us after all these years," Paula Patoka, Sandra Bertola's sister, told the Milwaukee Journal Sentinel. "This isn't going to end until she is found. It's an open wound. We're going to pursue this until we find her."

Private investigator Gerry Broderick appeared at his wits end. "There's no doubt in my mind who's responsible for this," Broderick told reporter Lisa Sink. How this guy can live with himself is quite beyond me. I hope he knows this is never going away. It's going to be with him until he dies." According to Broderick, the suspect did not provide a complete alibi on the night Sandra Bertolas disappeared. "He has pretty much stonewalled" investigators, said Broderick, currently a member of the Milwaukee County Board.

In October 2002, Waukesha County DA Paul Bucher told a reporter from the Milwaukee Journal Sentinel that finding Sandra's body might be the most important accomplishment of his career. "I want to do that so bad that I can taste it," said Bucher, who has since moved into private practice.

Similar to the disappearance of Jimmy Hoffa, theories exist about the location of Sandra Bertolas' body. Chances are that only one person knows, and he seems more than willing to carry this secret to his grave.

WISE MEN LET DEAD WISE GUYS LIE

JANUARY 13, 2010 | FILED UNDER ORGANIZED CRIME

Americans seem fascinated by stories of organized crime figures, especially those that focus on Italian crime families. The colorful monikers — the Weasel, Ice Pick, the Dapper Don — coupled with acts of brazen crimes, enables individuals with typically mundane routines to live precariously through others.

Over the last 15 years, several good works regarding organized crime have hit bookstore shelves. Some, like one of my favorites, Kill the Irishman, are an investigator's anthology of sorts featuring organizational charts linking the activities of various La Cosa Nostra groups throughout the United States.

With the activities of the mob curtailed dramatically by federal prosecutors using enhanced racketeering statutes, some authors are now revisiting the days of yore, sifting through documents and hatching new theories concerning well-known murders.

Scheduled for release this spring, once such book, Get Capone, purports that a Chicago businessman, linked at the hip to organized crime, is the man responsible for bringing down Al Capone; thereby, marginalizing the legend of Elliot Ness. Moreover, since the businessman is of the same ethnicity as Edward Burke, Chicago's 14th district alderman is using the new book's conclusions to scrub the reputation of Edward J. O'Hare.

Burke, whose crusade 13 years ago cleared Mrs. O'Leary's cow from igniting the Great Chicago Fire, is also seeking the assistance of the Chicago Police Department's cold case unit.

Gunned down as he drove his car near on Ogden Avenue over 70 years ago, Edward J. O'Hare was a business partner of Al Capone's. Until recently, some believed that allies of Capone—with the understanding that the mobster would soon be released from a stint at Alcatraz federal prison—committed the murder to free up funds from Sportsman's Park, a racetrack owned by O'Hare with Capone as a silent partner.

"Prohibition was over," the book's author Jonathan Elg told the Chicago Sun-Times. "The old outfit was earning at a fraction of its peak, but Eddie O'Hare was still making money at his racetracks..."

Burke alleges that O'Hare ratted out Capone by providing the government with the codes needed to crack his books. In return, O'Hare may have cooperated with the government to gain his son, Edward "Butch" O'Hare, entrance to the U.S. Naval Academy.

A Medal of Honor winner, the younger O'Hare became a Navy pilot who later lost his life in firefight with Japanese Zeros. His name now graces one of the busiest airports in the world.

Nevertheless, is it prudent to spend one iota of time reviewing a case whose suspects are likely deceased? After all, there are hundreds of other investigations more worthy of a cold case detective's time.

"History deserves that there be a true depiction of what happened," Burke told the Chicago Sun-Times."

True, although a resolution in this instance requires the attention of a researcher rather than an already overworked investigator.

BLACK AND WHITE CLOUD OF RETALIATION: PART I

JANUARY 17, 2010 | FILED UNDER ORGANIZED CRIME

As I mentioned in the previous post, Wise Men Let Dead Wise Guys Lie, federal prosecutors using enhanced racketeering laws have dealt significant blows to La Costa Nostra operatives in the United States. Although traditional Italian crime families receive the lion's share of attention from Hollywood, another group is beginning to get noticed — outlaw motorcycle gangs (OMG).

An FX Networks' television drama, Sons of Anarchy, tells the story of a Charming, California based outlaw motorcycle gang. Admittedly, I have never watched an episode of the show. Having witnessed the antics of OMG's first hand in Milwaukee, why anyone would want to romanticize these thugs is beyond comprehension.

The outlaw motorcycle idiom is a derivative of a July 4, 1947, Gypsy Tour motorcycle event held in Hollister, California. Over 4,000 motorcycle enthusiasts, as well as a dozen motorcycle clubs, including the Booze Fighters, the Top Hatters, and the Pissed of Bastards of Bloomington, packed the Bolado racetrack near the city's outskirts.

It was events in the town's center, however, that forever etched the surly image of bad boy bikers in the minds of mainstream society.

Sponsored by the American Motorcycle Association (AMA), the number of bikers in attendance — almost the equivalent of Hollister's population at the time — overwhelmed authorities. Over the July 4 weekend, fights, motorcycle accidents, and other acts of drunken hooliganism resulted in nearly 50 arrests and 60 injuries. Soon, photos of intoxicated bikers filled newspapers and appeared, albeit staged, in Life Magazine.

In response to the media attention, the secretary of the AMA, Lin Kuchler, stated, "The disreputable cyclists were possibly one-percent of the total number of motorcyclists; only one percent are hoodlums and troublemakers."

Outlaw bikers quickly seized on the label and, to this day, proudly don "1%" patches and tattoos.

In the United States, five major one-percent motorcycle gangs dominate the landscape: the Banditos, the Hells Angels, the Mongols, the Outlaws, and the Pagans. Smaller one-percent clubs exist, but one of the big-five organizations typically influences their activities.

Wisconsin is one of the few states still dominated primarily by the Outlaws Motorcycle Club. Since the early 1970s, the Outlaws MC has engaged in acts of violence in order to maintain its grip throughout the state. Problems tend to arise when motorcycle clubs within Wisconsin refuse to submit to the demands of the Outlaws or when clubs from outside the state encroach. During ensuing skirmishes, innocent persons, as well as members of other motorcycle clubs, end-up dead or seriously injured.

In early 1973, law enforcement sources received word that the Milwaukee chapter of the Outlaws was pressuring smaller one-percent clubs to drop their patches. In exchange, the Outlaws permitted a select number of the smaller clubs' members to 'patch-over' and become Outlaws. This edict did not sit well with the members of the Heaven's Devils, a local Milwaukee motorcycle club formed in the 1960s. When the Heaven's Devils refused to relinquish their patches, a handful of violent acts spilled over into the public arena.

In April 1974, two Outlaws committed a daring robbery at the residence of a Heaven's Devils member. The Outlaws took club patches from five Heaven's Devils.

In the world of one-percent bikers, losing a club's colors to a rival is tantamount to an act of cowardice, which may subject the errant biker to a beating by his own club's own members.

Outnumbered, the Heaven's Devils sought redress through the court system — taboo in the one-percent subculture. The HD's president ordered his members to testify against the Outlaws or risk expulsion from the club. These cooperating witnesses enabled the Milwaukee County District Attorney's office to obtain convictions, which resulted in the two Outlaws receiving seven-year prison terms.

NEXT: The retaliation begins with tragic consequences.

BLACK AND WHITE CLOUD OF RETALIATION: PART II

JANUARY 21, 2010 | FILED UNDER ORGANIZED CRIME

In 1974, after two members of the Milwaukee Outlaws robbed five rivals of the Heaven's Devils of their club's colors at gunpoint, the victims reported the brazen crime to officials from the Milwaukee Police Department. Michael Vermilyea, the President of the Heaven's Devils, stepped forward and agreed to testify. As a result, two Outlaws received seven-year prison terms. Living on the fringes of society, the Outlaws were livid.

Soon, the homes of a handful of Heaven's Devils members became targets for errand gunshots and firebombs. Vermilyea's residence wasn't spared, as a shotgun blast shattered the picture window of his home.

Unwilling to budge, some members of the Heaven's Devils held fast—refusing to drop their patches. When rival gangs feud, however, innocent parties sometimes find themselves caught in the middle.

On November 5, 1974, a young paperboy inadvertently stumbled into an escalation of violence. With a Milwaukee Sentinel carrying bag slung over his shoulder, 15-year-old Larry Anstett tossed papers onto the stoops of customer's homes in the 3200 block of N. 83 Street, a neatly kept blue-collar neighborhood on Milwaukee's northwest side. As he walked the sidewalk in the cool morning air, the ninth grade student eyed a small, colorfully wrapped package resting on the roof of a 1971 Oldsmobile. Standing on the driver's side of the car, Anstett picked-up the package, which immediately exploded in his face. Death was instantaneous.

Fragments of spent wielding rods shot through Anstett's body tearing apart his lungs, slicing his windpipe, blowing-off both hands, shattering bones in both arms, ripping the right eye from its socket, and burning the young boy's face beyond recognition.

The explosive device, the Heaven's Devils president told authorities, was meant for kill him—an early Christmas gift from the Outlaws—not Anstett. Contacted by a reporter from the Milwaukee Sentinel, Vermilyea wasted little time pointing fingers. "They [the Outlaws] knew where I lived, and an innocent kid got killed."

Intimidated by the Outlaws propensity for violence, potential witnesses refused to come forward. Although police did obtain a description of a two men leaving the area in pickup truck, the investigation quickly turned cold.

Several years later, an informant in a bind provided some critical information. He explained that the former "enforcer" of the Milwaukee Outlaws, John Buschman, and he burglarized a quarry in Lannon, Wisconsin — a small town ten miles west of Milwaukee — about four months prior to the Anstett homicide. The two men removed explosives and blasting caps and then stored them in a nearby barn. The informant later observed Buschman packing a cardboard box with pieces of metal and the explosives, which the Outlaw explained was a "present" for the Heaven's Devils.

The day of Larry Anstett's death, the informant visited a chop shop, where Buschman explained that a "kid" discovered the bomb, intended for president of the Heaven's Devil's.

The grisly killing of a young paperboy became the talk of the town. Clearly, the heat was on. Potential witnesses existed: two men left the scene of the bombing in pickup; the informant said a woman provided Buschman with detailed information about the explosives being stored at the quarry; and the informant himself observed Buschman packaging the "present."

Even though several years passed, the evidence seemed to point towards John Buschman.

NEXT: Christmas with the Outlaws

BLACK AND WHITE CLOUD OF RETALIATION: PART III

JANUARY 23, 2010 | FILED UNDER ORGANIZED CRIME

Over the years, the Outlaws, as well as other one-percent motorcycle clubs across the country, cultivated an image of a group of misunderstood, hard partying, rebel rousing, counterculture types searching for the next stretch of open road. In Milwaukee, that image dramatically changed when an improvised explosive device took the life of Larry Anstett, a 15-year-old newspaper delivery boy.

The feud between the Milwaukee chapter of the Outlaws Motorcycle Club and the Heaven's Devils soon became front-page news. For the first time, many members of the public—oblivious to the one-percent biker subculture—discovered that the carefree, live-and-let live depiction of bikers portrayed in the movie Easy Rider was a fantasy created by Hollywood movie producers.

But as the investigation into Larry Anstett's death turned cold, the Outlaws' ongoing war with the Heaven's Devils continued for another half-decade, for the most part, out of the public eye.

That changed in the early morning hours of December 16, 1979, when the Outlaws decided to crash the Heaven's Devils annual Christmas party. The event took place at the Knew Boot — a hole in the wall tavern located on the corner of S. 44th and W. Mitchell Streets in the tiny village of West Milwaukee.

Earlier in the evening, about 30 employees of the Milwaukee Sentinel made the trek from their company's Turner Hall Christmas party in downtown Milwaukee to the Knew Boot, where the working-class saloon offered shots and cocktails one could afford on a journalist's salary.

Soon after the Outlaws entered the tavern, all hell broke loose. One biker brandished a handgun, shots rang out and, after the smoke cleared, paramedics treated the casualties. John T. Janke, known to his fellow Heaven's Devils members as "Ox," lay dead and two additional Heaven's Devils sustained serious injuries.

Once again, employees from the Milwaukee Sentinel — the same newspaper Larry Anstett delivered — were caught in middle. Reporter John Tracy, 40, took a bullet to the head. He stayed at the scene and gave statements to investigators. Conveyed to St. Luke's Hospital, Tracy's brain swelled and he later slipped into a coma. Assistant picture editor Paul Rieger, 27, caught a round in his abdomen.

The investigation focused primarily on two members of the Outlaws, Gilbert Aspuro, 26, and 31-year-old Regan Murray. Witnesses alleged that Asparo ran-up to Heaven's Devil Allen Kurtz, placed a gun against his neck, and fired a shot. Murray fired five shots in the direction of Tracy, Reiger, and Janke. A witness told detectives that Janke's head snapped back after the shots, where he collapsed on to a chair and died. The ruckus started after a member of the Outlaws, Clifford Nowak, purposely dumped a drink on a rival biker.

Aspuro fled and headed to a friend's home in Fond du Lac, about 60 miles north of Milwaukee. Susan Lundgren told investigators that Asparo watched television news accounts of the shooting. After seeing the suspects' descriptions, Aspuro shaved his beard and mustache before cutting his hair.

Obtaining the evidence required to prosecute was difficult. This time, however, the Milwaukee County Sheriff's Office found witnesses willing to step forward. In April 1980, the Milwaukee County District Attorney's office launched a John Doe probe, which resulted in the issuance of five criminal counts, including party to the crime of first-degree murder.

"A bullet had entered the front of my head and lodged in the back," John Tracy described his injuries in a January 1, 1981, column in the Milwaukee Sentinel. The pressure from the injury caused his brain to swell and doctors told his family that, "they had given up, there wasn't anything more they could do for me." Tracy beat the odds and bounced back, but had difficulties recalling his own name and other simple words.

Regan Murray pled guilty to manslaughter and conduct regardless of life. He received a 22-year prison term. The DA's office dismissed the indictment against Aspuro after he passed a polygraph examination.

A few years later, unwilling to deal with the intimidation, threats and shootings, the Heaven's Devils dropped their patches and headed off into the sunset. The black and white cloud of retaliation—the colors the Outlaws proudly display—had claimed at least three innocent victims, while Larry Anstett's killer remained at large.

NEXT: Knowing where the skeletons are buried.

BLACK AND WHITE CLOUD OF RETALIATION: PART IV

JANUARY 26, 2010 | FILED UNDER ORGANIZED CRIME

Even as the feud between the Outlaws Motorcycle Club and the Heaven's Devils wound down, investigators doggedly worked to bring those responsible for the murder of 15-year-old Larry Anstett to justice. The problem with the case was a lack of corroborating witnesses.

After the blast on that chilly morning on November 5, 1974, the bomb's intended target, Heaven's Devils President Michael Vermilyea, quickly ran outside his home to assess the damage. The roof of his 1971 Oldsmobile had crumbled. Lying face down in the street was the lifeless paperboy. A witness told police that two men had fled in a pick-up truck.

A few years later, a man in a jam turned police informant. He told investigators that John Buschman, the purported enforcer of the Milwaukee Outlaws at the time of the Anstett homicide, burglarized a quarry to procure TNT. A few weeks prior to the bombing, the informant visited a farm in Sussex, Wisconsin; where he found Bushman, Outlaws' associate Joe Stoll, and Stoll's girlfriend. Buschman pointed to a package and told the informant it was a "present" for the Heaven's Devils.

Later on the day of the bombing, the informant observed Bushman and Stoll seated together in a pick-up truck that matched the description of the vehicle leaving the scene on N. 83rd Street. The following day, Joe Stoll and his girlfriend disappeared. Four years after the Anstett homicide, the farm's owner, Clifford Machan—a man contemplating a role as a state's witness—also vanished.

With several probable witnesses missing and likely dead, clearing the case proved difficult.

Police later recovered a body believed to be Machan's on a Waukesha County farm, while a key witnesses to his murder, Willy Cresca, passed away in August 2003 during a stint in the Waukesha County jail.

"Cresca helped bury the body [of Machan]," retired Milwaukee Police Department Detective Roger Hinterthuer told Milwaukee Journal Sentinel reporter Jacqueline Seibel. "But as long as Paul Bucher is the district attorney of Waukesha County, this case is going nowhere."

Judging the merits of the case in his role as a prosecutor, Bucher believed Cresca's criminal record would significantly damage his creditability as a witness. The former district attorney ran unsuccessfully for Wisconsin Attorney General in 2004 and is currently a private practice attorney.

"You are not going to get nuns as witnesses in these cases," Hinterthuer countered.

In all likelihood, however, the opportunity to bring the killer of Larry Anstett to justice probably died with Cresca. Absent new evidence, the case file will continue to collect dust.

Meanwhile, the former Milwaukee Outlaws' Club enforcer — the man Hinterhuer believes is responsible for as many as four homicides — remains a free man.

Absent a prosecution as a deterrent, members of the Outlaws continued their murderous ways documented during a round of racketeering indictments in the 1990s.

TO DEATH DO US PART?

FEBRUARY 25, 2010 | FILED UNDER COP TALK

About a week ago, I happened to run into a retired, former colleague at an over priced coffee shop. For about twenty minutes, we reminisced about "the job" — a term law enforcement officers use in reference to their profession, as if there is no other. Long retired, one vivid memory, it seemed, had burned its way into his mind.

Before proceeding further, I would describe this former officer as crusty, rough around the edges, a man's man, and a cop's cop. To put it mildly, no one would likely nominate this particular individual for Mr. Congeniality. Yet, years after the fact, it was evident that his memory still carried the burden of telling two caring parents that their teenaged child was no longer walking among the living.

During the course of their duties, investigators often serve as the grim reaper's official conduit to a next of kin. If one could only hear the mind of a detective en route to a death notification they would likely hear the clatter of different scenarios bouncing-off the walls of the brain searching for a way to explain—with some sense of decency—that the loved one who left for work or school just a few hours earlier will never return.

Although a supposed work of fiction, a chapter from Mitchell Nevin's book, The Cozen Protocol, sheds some light on the circumstances surrounding death notifications. Fleeing the scene of a gruesome homicide, a member of a Dominican drug cartel tossed the firearm used in the crime from a car window as his get-a-way vehicle traveled over a city bridge. A short time later, while exploring the banks of the nearly frozen river on his way home from school, a young boy found what he believed to be a toy, pointed the object at a friend, and pulled the trigger. Two homicide detectives later arrived at the deceased victim's home to make contact with his mother, explaining that her 12-year-old son was in transit to the Medical Examiner's office for an autopsy.

It has taken a while but police departments are now offering specialized training pertaining to these death notifications. In Canada, Lloyd Grahame, a retired member of the Windsor, Ontario Police Service, has developed a law enforcement-training program to ease the burden of officers involved in such duties.

Even though Canada has far fewer homicides per capita than the United States, our neighbor to the north has just as many drinkers, as the Canadian version of Mothers Against Drunk Driving sponsors Grahame's seminar. The training itinerary includes the fundamental elements of a death notification, dealing with the apprehensions of performing the process, identifying the needs of the next of kin, determining what is appropriate to say, and establishing a protocol for the viewing of the deceased by the bereaved.

In the past, budgetary issues permitted only a handful of officers and detectives to receive such training. Just recently, however, the Canadian Police Knowledge Network has made Grahame's program available online.

It is now feasible for law enforcement agencies to provide in-depth death notification training at the academy level. By doing so, this difficult process will no longer scare the memories of those who deliver terrible news to a next of kin.

SERIAL KILLER IN PLAIN SIGHT FOR ALL TO SEE

FEBRUARY 20, 2010 | FILED UNDER CONSPIRACY

Located along the shores of the Mississippi River, La Crosse, Wisconsin is a blue-collar town of about 113,000 with a tradition of hard drinking. The city is also home to the University of Wisconsin – La Crosse, a popular state college, and Viterbo University, a small, private Catholic liberal arts institution, with a total enrollment of more than 3,000 students.

Prior to Labor Day, about 13,000 college students — the equivalent of ten percent of La Crosse's population — make their annual pilgrimage to campus. Like many other college towns throughout the country, students under the legal drinking age find their way to house parties or occasionally sneak into taverns.

Yet the culture of binge drinking in La Crosse differs from other college towns. Since 1997, nine men have drowned in the Mississippi River. All had two things in common: they were college students and all were inebriated.

The most recent death occurred about a week ago. Craig Meyers, a 21-year-old criminal justice student at Western Technical College, spent the early morning hours drinking at two La Crosse taverns after attending a wedding reception. A friend gave Meyers a ride to the area of 7th and Market Streets, one-half block west of Viterbo University. The next morning, a relative reported Myers missing.

Suspecting intoxication, the La Crosse police canvassed the area for witnesses. Checking a surveillance camera from the Sara Lee bakery, investigators found video of a man matching Meyers' description walking alone near 4th and Cass Streets, six blocks northeast of the drop-off point. A bloodhound traced Meyers scent to the Mississippi River. Police then found footprints on the thin ice that suddenly disappeared. Divers found Meyers' body two days later. His blood alcohol content registered .28, nearly three-and-a-half times the limit used to determine impaired driving.

Unfortunately, this story is an all too familiar one for La Crosse police, who have come under fire by conspiracy theorists suggesting that a serial killer, a rogue cop, or a seductive female is somehow responsible for these deaths.

The evidence be damned, some suspect foul play, which is why they go out of their way to bend the facts in order to implicate the infamous, although yet unidentified, 'smiley face' killer.

Conceived by retired New York City police detectives Kevin Gannon and Anthony Duarte in 2008, the 'smiley face' serial killer theory suggests an individual or group is roaming the United States on the lookout for intoxicated males walking near bodies of water. Ever since their investigation of the 1997 death of New York City college student Patrick O'Neil, the two detectives began monitoring similar occurrences.

As is often the case, conspiracy theories typically contain a shard of truth — just enough to allow believers to grab hold and refuse to let go. The death investigation of 21-year-old Christopher Jenkins provided such fodder for the advocates of the 'smiley face' serial killer scenario.

On October 31, 2001, Jenkins celebrated Halloween with his girlfriend, Ashley Rice, at the Lone Tree Bar and Grill in downtown Minneapolis. A bouncer, the last person to see him alive, later escorted Jenkins from of the tavern absent his jacket or wallet. A University of Minnesota student, Jenkins' disappearance was similar to the deaths in La Crosse, as well as two others in the Minneapolis area, which authorities quickly linked to alcohol consumption.

Four months later, a citizen observed Jenkins' body, caught on some branches in Mississippi River near the Horseshoe Dam, still clad in his American Indian costume. Minneapolis police listed the cause of death as "unknown," although investigators suspected an accidental drowning or suicide.

Unlike the police, Steve and Jan Jenkins suspected foul play had a role in their son's death. They hired a private investigator to look into the matter. After viewing photographs of Jenkins still in the water, former detectives Gannon and Duarte believed the position of the body and other physical evidence suggested Jenkins did not die accidentally.

Then, in the fall of 2006, Sgt. Pete Jackson, of the Minneapolis Police Department, received a call.

"A source brought me a rumor," Jackson told Minnesota Public Radio. "Just a faint rumor of something they'd heard — that somebody said somebody said something. It was about tenth-hand. And at that point I decided I needed to just kind of go and take a look at this. Because prior to that we really had no idea, really, how Chris ended up in the river."

Minneapolis police now believe they know how Christopher Jenkins fell into the Mississippi River. They even have a suspect, a man held on other charges. According to Sgt. Jackson, the "eyewitness slash suspect" provided specific information relevant to the crime scene.

While Minneapolis police have released few details, the rumor mill has it that the suspect may have had an interest in Jenkins' girlfriend.

While 'smiley face' killer theorists are quick to point to Christopher Jenkins as proof that the police are too quick to write-off these drowning deaths as accidental, investigators have not linked the suspect to any additional cases, even though detectives have examined the suspect's whereabouts and compared them to their investigative timelines.

Back in La Crosse, the serial killer allegations and the finger pointing at the police department have brought about a three-year crackdown on underage drinking. Some students claim police initiate contact with youthful looking citizens while walking in certain parts of town and ask to search their backpacks.

The baseless allegations of a police cover-up appear to have riled La Crosse Police Chief Edward Kondracki.

"The previous river drownings have all been thoroughly investigated and reinvestigated by the Wisconsin Division of Criminal Investigation and La Crosse Police Department, with a review by the Federal Bureau of Investigation," said Kondracki in a written statement. "There is no serial killer!

"Police officers and (Operation) River Watch volunteers have saved over fifty people in recent years who were either in the water, or on the edge of, or attempting suicide in the river. Some cases are nearly identical to this case."

I, too, believe there is possible, high-ranking suspect behind the drowning deaths of these young men. His picture is there for all to see, in plain sight — on a bottle of Captain Morgan

MAX & THE MOB

APRIL 24, 2010 | FILED UNDER ORGANIZED CRIME

From the 1930s through the late 1980s, colorful characters peppered Milwaukee's traditional organized crime scene. The movie Donnie Brasco, starring Al Pacino and Johnny Depp, chronicles the story of Joe Pistone, an FBI agent who successfully infiltrated the New York City based Bonanno crime family. In his book, Pistone provides details of a stop in Milwaukee, along with his capo, Benjamin "Lefty" Ruggiero. The two New Yorkers visited the city's eastside, where Frank Balistrieri, the leader of the Milwaukee mob, held court at Snug's Restaurant inside the Shorecrest Hotel.

The federal government's 1983 indictment of Frank Balistrieri was the beginning of the end of Milwaukee's La Cosa Nostra connection, although other organized crime figures remained on the radar screen of federal authorities and detectives from the Milwaukee Police Department.

One such individual was Max Adonnis.

Organized crime investigators often claim that the lower the profile of a Mafioso the higher the rank. If this theory holds true, then Adonnis, at best, held a low-level status. Born Maxmillan Ludwig Gajewski, he changed his last name to represent himself as Italian, even though the origin of the name Adonnis is a Greek derivative.

Born in May of 1935, the first blurb on Adonnis' rap sheet appeared on July 4, 1953; a court found him guilty of disorderly conduct and fined $5. From 1963 to 1965, he dabbled in worthless checks. By August of 1971, Milwaukee police arrested Adonnis for false imprisonment and aggravated battery for kidnapping a man who stole items from an associate. These are the usual offenses committed by two-bit thugs, even though Adonnis managed to committed offenses having only one arm.

In 1976, Adonnis, then the maitre d' at Sally's Steak House, located at 1028 E. Juneau Street, was convicted of conspiracy to commit extortion and theft after efforts were made to collect on payments for restaurant owner Sally Papia, who, police sources claim, also had connections to organized crime figures.

After his employment at Sally's, Adonnis accepted a position as the maitre d' and general manager at Giovanni's Restaurant, where reports soon surfaced linking him to cocaine trafficking. Operated by Giovanni and Rosa Safina, the restaurant itself, based, in part, on Adonnis' presence, caused former Milwaukee County District Attorney E. Michael McCann to declare the premise off-limits for members of his staff. As it became apparent that Adonnis' enemies knew where they could find him, McCann's ban proved prudent.

On a sunny afternoon on April 10, 1985, Paul Waterman took a stroll along E. Brady Street after being dropped-off by his father to visit relatives. The 29-year-old then observed the one-armed man he recognized from an incident almost two-decades earlier — the home invasion of his childhood residence. Present during the attack, the trauma of the event, Waterman claimed, caused him to develop life altering, violent seizures.

But as Waterman approached his nemesis, it became clear that Adonnis had no clue with whom he was dealing with.

"Hey, you fat bastard!" Waterman yelled, as he confronted the pudgy, one-armed man in front of 623 E. Brady Street.

When the target of the slur took offense, Waterman removed a four-inch knife and stabbed Adonnis twice to the left and right abdominal areas. One incision came just centimeters from the heart. Waterman then fled on foot; however, officers soon apprehended him at gunpoint, after he threw the knife used in the stabbing to the ground, in the 800 block of E. Pearson Street.

Paramedics rushed Adonnis to Milwaukee County General Hospital for surgery. He survived the attack, although it became clear that a growing list of enemies had painted a target on Adonnis' back.

A year later, detectives learned that Adonnis was driving a blue Rolls Royce registered to Rosa Safina. Investigators learned that Safina had borrowed $50,000 to pay for the vehicle, even though Adonnis appeared to one operating the car. In July of 1987, word leaked that Adonnis maintained a property on Eagle Lake in Racine County, although the Safina family officially owned the property.

As a maitre d' and general manager for a small, family-owned restaurant, Adonnis apparently did very well for himself. This, of course, caused investigators to speculate that Adonnis had access to black market income.

Yet even some black market income — according to the unwritten rules of the vice underground — is illicitly obtained, as are the methods employed to retrieve ill-gotten proceeds.

On February 28, 1989, someone totting a 12 gauge shotgun fired five rounds into Adonnis' 1988 Lincoln Town Car parked in the 700 block of E. Brady Street. According the victim, he had no idea who the suspects may be or why persons would target him. But the writing on the wall suggested that Adonnis' life in the fast lane was about to come to a screeching halt, either through a long stint in prison or by an ever growing list of grudge holders.

Reality came to fruition on March 18, 1989. An out of town couple happened into the parking lot of Giovanni's Restaurant in search of hot breakfast but, instead, caught a glimpse of a cleaning woman fleeing the restaurant bleeding from the neck. Inside, police discovered Max Adonnis dead with a gunshot wound to the head. According the cleaning woman, the suspects were both African-American.

"Sources said Adonnis had been very nervous and shaken," wrote Milwaukee Sentinel reporters Mary Zahn and Lori Sklitzky, "since a Feb. 28 incident in which his car was riddled with gunshot pellets near his home at 706 E. Brady Street." The reporters further noted that the two men who fled after the shooting "knew Adonnis and had been in the restaurant several days before the murder." News accounts linked Adonnis to a south side cocaine trafficker, who had visited Giovanni's Restaurant on several occasions.

Almost a month after the homicide, police had yet to affect and arrest. Evidence surfaced when a man found a plastic garbage bag containing items belonging to Adonnis on the banks of the Milwaukee River behind the A.F. Fallun & Sons Co. tannery, located just a quarter mile from the crime scene. Otherwise, the investigation ran cold.

Almost two years later, detectives discovered the bodies of two African-American males buried beneath a basement of a home at 941 S. 35th Street. Speculation mounted that the home's owner may have connections to organized crime and that the bodies were those of the suspects in the Adonnis murder.

"Sources said the day the bodies were recovered," wrote Milwaukee Journal reporter Anne Bothwell, "an informant told police they would find the bodies under the basement, and that the victims were the killers of restaurateur and crime figure Maximillion J. Adonnis."

A few weeks later, police arrested two men, Scott Heimermann, 30, and Edward Piscitello, 37, for the slayings of 23-year-old Muhammad Bin-Walee and Dion V. Russell, 17. Bin-Walee was a member of the Brothers of the Struggle, a violent north side street gang—an offshoot of the Chicago based Gangster Disciples. Investigators later discarded the theory that connected these murders the Adonnis homicide.

Max Adonnis was "an old-school 'crook' who lived by a code of honor," an anonymous police source told the Milwaukee Sentinel shortly after the restaurateur's death. "He was probably one of the last of his kind. He kept that old code of silence. He wasn't a snitch."

In reality, karma caught-up with Max Adonnis—a one-armed block bully who lived by the sword and died by the sword.

DID DAHMER DO IT?

APRIL 1, 2010 | FILED UNDER TRUE CRIME

On March 28, Miami Herald reporters David Smiley and Arthur J. Harris revisited the case of Adam Walsh, a six-year-old boy who went missing from a Hollywood, Florida Sears Store in 1981. Even though this investigation is nearly 30-years-old, the young boy's disappearance and subsequent homicide remains one of our nation's highest profile crimes, due, in part, to the relentless perseverance of Adam's father, John Walsh, the host of America's Most Wanted.

In late 2008, the Hollywood, Florida Police Department conclusively linked Adam's death to Otis Toole, a drifter claiming to have committed several dozen homicides in conjunction with his lover, Henry Lee Lucas. Beginning in 1983, investigators from a number of jurisdictions obtained confessions from either Toole or Lucas only to learn that many were outright fabrications.

Because of these bogus confessions, skeptics in the media are revisiting homicide cases that investigators have written-off as cleared. The Miami Herald's Smiley and Harris, citing the decades-old recollections of a handful of witnesses, now believe Milwaukee serial killer Jeffrey Dahmer may have had a hand in Adam Walsh's death.

In July 1981, after his discharge from the Army for alcoholism, Dahmer found employment at Sunshine Subs, located a few miles away from the scene of Adam Walsh's abduction. The shop's supervisor at the time told the reporters that Dahmer had access to a blue delivery van similar to the illegally parked vehicle one witness, Janice Santamassino, almost struck on July 27, 1981, outside the Sears store on the date of the young boy's disappearance.

While Adam Walsh's body, in total, was never located, police recovered his severed head from a drainage canal on August 10, 1981, adjacent to the Florida Turnpike. Two truck drivers contacted investigators the following day to report seeing a blue van parked near the site three days earlier. "Denis Bubb saw a man with a flashlight…," the reporters note. "Both [drivers] say they talked to Hollywood police and were told the incident had nothing to do with the Adam Walsh murder."

Smiley and Harris cite possible eyewitness identifications of Dahmer, many of which are almost three decades old. One such witness, Phillip Lohr, who claims to have seen a blue van outside the Sears toy department, failed to contact police until 1997.

The one obvious link to Dahmer is the severed head.

In 1991, Tracy Edwards flagged-down Milwaukee beat cops Mueller and Roth to report that a "weird dude" had put handcuffs on him while watching a video. Checking into the story, the officers gained entry to the now infamous apartment 213. Eleven severed heads and other body parts were located inside.

Edwards, a man many Milwaukee police officers frequently spotted in various inner city drug houses, was an adult, as were the vast majority of Dahmer's other murder victims, although Konerak Sinthasomphone was nearing his fifteenth birthday. Moreover, the investigation in Milwaukee found no evidence suggesting that Dahmer targeted small children.

Dahmer also maintained a large collection of photographs of victims, many of which depicted persons in various stages of dismemberment. Having seen these pictures, images of small children are noticeably absent. The photographs, like the severed heads, are key pieces of the puzzle. Serial killers often save souvenirs from victims to relive their bizarre fantasies. The Dahmer case gained national and international attention, yet, to the best of my knowledge, not a single memento was ever located linking Dahmer to a pre-teen homicide.

Another facet of the Walsh case that seems to exclude Dahmer is the lack of a confession. While in the custody of Milwaukee police, Dahmer, for the most part, confessed to his crimes.

The Miami Herald article notes that FBI agent Neil Purtell, who later interviewed the serial killer, believed Dahmer admitted killing Adam Walsh due to his "overly fervent denials." However, Dahmer later told Hollywood Detective Jack Hoffman that, "...he never killed children but didn't want to rot in prison and would admit to Adam's murder if it meant a death sentence." Regardless of how one interprets these statements, Dahmer did not implicate himself in Adam Walsh's death, even though he appeared to have a motive to do so.

As far as the Miami Herald article is concerned, the reporters deserve credit where credit is due. The bogus confessions of Toole and Lucas likely resulted in clearances of homicides that left the actual perpetrators at large to kill again. Off the top of my head, I am aware of three Wisconsin cases — the 1978-1980 Madison area homicides of Julie Speerschneider, Julie Ann Hall, and Shirley Stewart — that detectives believe Lucas committed. The Lucas and Toole homicide spree fallacies need debunking in order to prevent future crimes from occurring.

M.P.D. BLUE —
A PORTRAIT OF POLICE WORK

JUNE 27, 2010 | FILED UNDER COP TALK

As a lieutenant in the Milwaukee Police Department's homicide unit, Dave Kane had a reputation as a straight shooter who—in his passion for the job—didn't mince words. As such, I wasn't the least bit surprised to find Dave's new book, M.P.D. Blue, a no-nonsense saga of his 30 years of police service.

For those of you interested in police work, M.P.D. Blue is a must-read. Last week, Milwaukee Journal Sentinel columnist Jim Stingl profiled the book:

http://www.jsonline.com/news/milwaukee/96944404.html

Stingl focused on Kane's involvement as a supervisor during the Jeffrey Dahmer investigation and his infiltration—albeit brief—of the Ku Klux Klan. Without a doubt, these two stories are interesting to the general public. I, on other hand, having walked a mile in his shoes as lieutenant of detectives, enjoyed the darts Dave occasionally threw that hit their mark.

One chapter of the book, entitled The Cigarette Package, describes homicide detective Greg Schuler's attention to detail. After a citizen discovered a prostitute strangled to death in an alley near N. 27th Street and W. Fond du Lac Avenue, Kane and Schuler responded to the scene to investigate. Garbage and debris litter this notoriously seedy section of Milwaukee. The victim, a black female, was partially disrobed and had a wooden stick shoved in her vagina. In the midst of the clutter, Schuler had to decipher which pieces of litter had the potential for evidentiary value. One of the items Schuler collected from amongst the debris was a crusty cigarette package.

A few days later, Schuler called Kane to explain that an evidence technician developed a latent fingerprint from the cigarette pack that belonged to a young male living in the area.

"You mean to tell me," Kane quotes himself telling Schuler, "that you picked up a cigarette pack at the [garbage filled] scene?" Schuler explained that, having examined the filthy alley, he believed the suspect might have dropped the package. A short time thereafter, Schuler had a suspect in custody who confessed to the crime.

Within the scope of two days, Schuler had cleared two homicides with confessions. Kane was so appreciative of the detective's work that he nominated Schuler for the Milwaukee Police Department's Superior Achievement Award. Months later, however, Kane explains, the award went to "a uniformed sergeant for devising a plan that saved the department two reams of copy paper. But that was the Milwaukee Police Department. The CIB [the detective bureau] was viewed as the bastard child sometimes."

In M.P.D. Blue, Kane writes of an incident where he came just inches from losing his life. On November 13, 1970, Kane and his partner, Dick Shannon, conducted a traffic stop for a defective taillight.

As Kane handed the driver, Lee Seward, a releasable citation for an equipment violation, he observed what he believed to be a flash bulb popping and initially thought a firecracker had exploded; however, within a few seconds, it became clear that someone had fired a shot. The two beat cops ran back to their squad, backed-up a short distance, and radioed a call of "shots fired."

As a cop involved in a few similar situations, hearing dozens of sirens responding is indeed a Godsend.

What occurred next, though, was difficult for the two officers to decipher. The passenger of the vehicle, a Ford convertible, exited and lay prone of the ground. They later discovered that a sniper with a .30-06 rifle took a shot at Kane, who was at the driver's side door.

Officers whisked Kane to the hospital to treat a graze wound to his arm.

"When I got to the hospital," Kane writes, "I noticed some peculiar substance sprayed all over the front of my coat. I would later learn that the substance was the exploded brain matter of Lee Seward. The bullet that had struck my arm had continued onward, striking Mr. Seward in the head as he sat in his car."

Of course, the passenger, believing the police had summarily executed the courteous driver for no apparent reason, exited to surrender.

The next day, two officers stopped Willie Triplett and Willie Campbell. A search of their vehicle turned-up the .30-06 used to kill Seward. The two teenaged-boys told investigators that they wanted to "kill a pig." A month earlier, the pair had shot and killed a security guard they believed was a police officer. Unknown to Kane's partner, a week prior to the death of Seward, the pair shot at Shannon's unoccupied squad. Investigators later discovered the round lodged under the vehicle's gas pedal.

M.P.D. Blue, a quick read well-worth its cost, is a collection of almost two dozen other interesting war stories.

THE MYSTERIOUS WHEREABOUTS OF RALPH LEON JACKSON

JUNE 13, 2010 | FILED UNDER TRUE CRIME

On April 7, 2010, Augusta (Virginia) County Sheriff's deputies surrounded the home of Ralph Leon Jackson. A short time thereafter, the 56-year-old mechanic was in police custody for the shooting of Timothy Davis, 27, at the Rock Point Overlook on the Blue Ridge Parkway. Augusta County Sheriff Randall Fisher later told the media that Jackson confessed to the crime.

During SF's visit to Virginia, a link analysis question arose. The tight-lipped investigation into Jackson's background—specifically his whereabouts on the dates of several brutal, unsolved homicides—has fueled speculation.

A media report published shortly after Jackson's arrest mentioned the homicides of David Metzler, 19, and Heidi Childs, 18, two Virginia Tech students shot to death at the Caldwell Fields Campground inside the Jefferson National Forrest. A passer-by discovered Metzler inside his 1992 Toyota, while Childs' body was located outside the vehicle. Absent ballistics information, one can only speculate that, as in the Davis shooting, the perpetrator used a shotgun — a possible nexus between the two crime scenes.

Speculation aside, court documents indicate that investigators obtained DNA from Jackson a few days after his arrest. While it may take months to stand in line for a possible hit from CODIS, the FBI's national DNA database, comparing a known sample directly to a specimen recovered from a particular crime scene can take just weeks. An educated guess is that officials from the Augusta County Sheriff's Department may already know if a link exists between the Metzler/Childs/Davis homicides. Since Childs' father is a member of law enforcement, you can bet the farm that solving this young woman's homicide is high priority.

As far as a possible link to the Colonial Parkway murders, the incident closest to the modus operandi of Jackson on the Blue Ridge Parkway is the September 1987 homicides of David Knobling, 20, and Robin Edwards, 14, at the Ragged Island Wildlife Refuge. However, the firearm used to gun-down the couple was not a shotgun. The Lauer/Phelps homicides are probable stabbing deaths, as are Thomas/Dowski. Furthermore, since it appears that Jackson's signature is leaving the victims at the scene, he is a very unlikely suspect in the Call/Hailey disappearance.

As investigators weave their way through the whereabouts of Ralph Leon Jackson, they are probably examining his travels along Virginia's Route 29, although the cause of Alicia Showalter Reynolds' 1996 death is not a public record. In an April 9, 2010, Spingola Files posting, I noted the similarities between Jackson and the composite sketch of the Route 29 suspect.

http://www.badgerwordsmith.com/spingolafiles/2010/04/09/a-break-in-the-case/

Initially, the Roanoke Times reported that the suspect in the shooting death of Davis stood 5 feet 8 inches tall, while witnesses put the man believed to be the Route 29 stalker at 5 feet 10 to six feet tall, 35 to 45 years-of-age, and about 180 pounds. In 1996, Jackson was 42-years-old. He currently undergoes aggressive chemotherapy to treat advanced prostate cancer, which may cause dramatic weight loss.

Is it possible that Jackson, having reportedly confessed to his involvement in the Blue Ridge Parkway shooting, is withholding information about other crimes so the state might forgo a capital murder prosecution?

Only time will tell.

Yet, from my experiences as a homicide detective, an agency's silence pertaining to a major murder investigation with a suspect in custody typically means that things are heating up. As far as Ralph Leon Jackson is concerned, investigators have already served subpoenas for bank records, vehicle repairs orders, credit card information, and cellular telephone data. Sifting through these materials and interviewing hundreds of people will take time. My guess is the public will hear more about Mr. Jackson on or near the 4th of July.

BAD WEEK TO BE BRITISH IN MADISON

JULY 2, 2010 | FILED UNDER HOMICIDE

High profile homicides sometimes become nightmares for law enforcement, especially when they involve participants from more than one agency. When the victim is an attractive white female, such as Natalee Holloway, JonBenet Ramsey, or Stacy Peterson, it seems that the level of media scrutiny increases exponentially.

Things get worse when an investigation is thrown-for-a-loop by the appearance of indolence and/or ineptitude, as well as the perception that public officials are using the courts to sweep a handful of embarrassing items under the proverbial government carpet.

Such a scenario unfolded in Madison, Wisconsin over two-years ago. Just after one-in-the-afternoon, when Jordan Gonnering discovered the corpse of his fiancé, 21-year-old University of Wisconsin student Brittany Zimmermann, inside the couple's lower-level apartment at 517 W. Doty Street. The bloody scene led Gonnering to believe the young woman succumbed to a gunshot wound.

Although the Dane County Coroner's report lists the cause of death as "complex homicidal violence," terminology often used to conceal the cause of death from the public, details listed in an affidavit note that Zimmermann died of multiple stab wounds to the chest and blunt force trauma to the head.

When investigators arrived, the already troubling murder case took a strange twist—one that would pit one governmental agency against another.

On April 2, 2008, at 12:20 p.m., Zimmermann dialed 911 from her cellular telephone. Rita Gahagan, an employee of the Dane County Emergency Dispatch Center, picked-up the call, which soon ended.

"The disconnect call started," according to a search warrant affidavit filed by Madison Police Department Detective Marion Morgan, "with the sound of a woman screaming and the line remains active and open picking up the background sounds of a struggle for a short period of time."

Instead of ascertaining the location of the call and dispatching Madison police, sources say Gahagan attempted to reestablish telephone contact with Zimmermann.

It was information from this attempt at re-contact that threw detectives from the Madison Police Department off the scent of the killer. Sources claim the 911 Center dialed the wrong number. A man with a noticeable British accent answered and truthfully reported that all was well.

Armed with this information, investigators spent five days scouring Madison for homeless or drug addicted men with British accents. So thorough was this dragnet that a handful of people matching this particular profile were, in fact, located and grilled.

Needless to say, it was a bad week to be British in Madison.

It was almost a week, however, before investigators learned that the 911 Center had contacted the wrong number. Detectives, having expended valuable time and resources chasing down a bad lead, now had to start from scratch.

Soon afterwards, officials from the Dane County 911 Center and the Madison Police Department began pointing fingers at each other. Absent a reading of the official police reports or having first hand knowledge of what transpired at the Doty Street crime scene, it is too difficult and unproductive to assess blame. That being said one of the first items on a homicide detective's agenda is obtaining the victim's telephone records—home and cellular. If investigators located Zimmermann's cellular telephone at the scene, a cursory examination would likely reveal recent incoming and outgoing calls. If the killer took the young woman's cell phone, investigators generally subpoena incoming and outgoing calls, text messages, and obtain GPS coordinates. Either way, within a matter of days, a prudent investigator would likely know if the 911 Center attempted to reestablish contact with Zimmermann's cell phone.

The dynamics of a fluid, probable stranger homicide investigation—coupled with the 911 Center misinformation—gives the impression that Dane County administrators are in all-out, butt-covering mode. Some even point fingers at the Madison Police Department, where a snafu resulted in the affidavit for the original search warrant being released to the media.

Unfortunately, Dane County Judge Maryann Sumi's June 30 ruling halting a negligence lawsuit brought by the Zimmermann family against Dane County and Gahagan has provided further fuel for the conspiracy theorists' fire. In instances of an ongoing criminal investigation, case law, as Judge Sumi correctly notes, is clear that the integrity of an open homicide case takes precedence over the release of discovery in civil matters.

Critics of Judge Sumi's ruling point out that some critical details pertaining to the Zimmermann homicide made their way into the public eye when information from the search warrant affidavit appeared in media reports. They believe the civil case could proceed by limiting the documents to those that may shed light on issues of culpability. Furthermore, there are some who believe that Dane County is a locale where the politically connected cover for each other. They view the judge's ruling, rightly or wrongly, as good-old-girl network stonewalling.

True, the mistaken release of the search warrant and its supporting affidavit in the Zimmerman investigation does make an argument for absolute restrictions on the release of civil case discovery less relevant. Yet, in this instance, the Dane County judiciary's unwillingness to seal sensitive search warrants indefinitely is as much of an issue as the debacle relating to the release itself. In Milwaukee County, where the courts recognize that detectives have their hands full, judges seal search warrants indefinitely when cause presents itself. Parties with a particular interest in the disclosure of these documents can, if they so choose, petition the court for disclosure.

In the interim, Madison police continue to investigate the Zimmermann homicide by casting lines into the ever-expanding DNA pond. The betting money says that their profile of the probable killer—a likely unemployed transient with a drug problem—is right on the mark.

WHEN JUSTICE IS AS BLIND AS ITS WITNESSES

NOVEMBER 13, 2010 | FILED UNDER HOMICIDE

Imagine this scenario: you are a police officer in small, Midwestern town. On a typical afternoon, a slew of fellow law enforcement officers knock on your door with guns drawn. Probably believing those in blue have the wrong address; you answer, and soon find yourself under arrest for homicide.

A few hours later, investigators hold a line-up at the county jail and a witness identifies you as the killer.

Soon, two law enforcement agencies in different states participate in a news conference. The leaders of these organizations pat each others' back and thank their detectives for snagging the perpetrator in short order.

So willing to take whatever the government provides them at face value, the media explores your background. The press speaks to relatives and friends, and even scrutinizes the contents of your Facebook page.

Of course, the word "allegedly" prefaces the media's coverage, even though they believe that you are as guilty as sin. Some media types even lead with a paragraph strongly indicating a presumption of guilt.

"Relatives and coworkers of a small-town police officer charged in a Midwestern shooting spree that killed one man and wounded two others say they're baffled by the cop's bizarre behavior and arrest," wrote contributor from AOL News, concluding, in a de facto sense, that the police officer is the perpetrator.

And there you sit, stuck in a Joliet, Illinois jail with some of the same people that you might have sent-up the river.

But it gets worse. Based solely on eyewitness identifications, the district attorney files a murder charge. Bail is set at $2.5 million.

While this scenario may seem far-fetched it became a reality for Lynwood, Illinois Police Officer Brian Dorian.

In early October, a man—similar in appearance to Dorian—approached a group of construction workers in the rural community of Beecher, Illinois, shooting and killing a 45-year-old man and wounding another. Less than an hour later, the same man approached a farmer in the Indiana border town of Lowell, and inquired about honeybees stored on the property. The man then shot the farmer and fled in a pick-up truck.

After his arrest, Dorian, hoping to convince investigators of his innocence, did the best he could to account for his whereabouts on the date of the shootings—to no avail.

Then detectives, having seized Dorian's computer, realized that their county's prosecutor had charged an innocent man with murder. Using the digital recovery program Encase, forensic examiners discovered that, on the date and time of the homicide in Beecher, Dorian had logged on to the Internet and was visiting a password specific Web site.

Soon afterwards, the district attorney's office dropped the charges against Dorian.

Then the finger pointing began.

Detectives claimed Dorian failed to supply them with the information regarding his computer use on the date of the shootings.

Realistically, though, how many Americans, if asked, would specifically recall what they were doing a week prior? Sure, some individuals could say, with certainty, they were at work or school, but what if they were on vacation or, like Dorian, laid-up due to an injury?

Think about it: where would Brian Dorian be today if he had not logged on to Internet during one of the shootings?

In the criminal justice system, misidentifications are the primary cause for wrongful convictions.

The Innocence Project notes that, "Seventy-five percent of wrongful convictions overturned with DNA testing involve eyewitness misidentification."

In Reevaluating Lineups: Why Witnesses Make Mistakes, the Innocence Project found that in 50 percent of the misidentification cases eyewitness testimony was the central evidence used against the defendant. In 38 percent of the instances involving wrongful convictions based on misidentifications, "multiple eyewitnesses misidentified the same innocent person."

In several instances, the Innocence Project's research illustrates that photo arrays and lineups failed to include fillers of persons that resembled the suspect.

As a result, witnesses identified the lineup participant that—based on a process of elimination—looked closest to the actual perpetrator.

In Brain Dorian's case, investigators used a photo array and a lineup, as well as the description of Dorian's truck, as probable cause for the homicide charge. Clearly, the eyewitnesses and investigators got it wrong, but, I believe, had Dorian's computer failed to provide the proof necessary to exonerate him, these same witnesses would have appeared in court and sternly fingered Dorian as the shooter.

Reports are now surfacing that Dorian's nightmare has traumatized him to the point that he no longer can serve. According to the Chicago Sun-Times, Dorian's boss, Lynwood police Chief Russell Pearson, has this advice for his wrongfully charged officer: sue.

"I told them (Will County Sheriff's Department Investigators) they were making a big mistake," Pearson told Sun-Times reporter Joe Hosey. "They said they had evidence, which apparently they did not."

Reading between the lines, Will County investigators and the charging District Attorney's office do not appear too overly concerned that they had wrongfully arrested an exemplary officer without adequately processing the physical evidence.

The rush to judgment in the Dorian investigation is eerily reminiscent of the charges brought against Raymond Donovan, the Reagan administration's Secretary of Labor, who after a jury acquitted him of larceny and fraud charges, asked the media, "Which office do I go to get my reputation back?"

THE HONEYBEE SHOOTER CASE: CIRCUMSTANCE OR COINCIDENCE?

NOVEMBER 18, 2010 | FILED UNDER HOMICIDE

Black's Law Dictionary describes circumstantial evidence as "evidence in a trial which is not directly from an eyewitness or participant and requires some reasoning to prove a fact."

A seasoned courtroom observer would likely explain that circumstantial evidence is the presentation of several smaller pieces of a much larger puzzle in the hopes that a jury will believe—absent the primary components—that an overwhelming probability exists that a defendant committed the charged offense.

The problem with circumstantial evidence is that a series of facts can point toward guilt, even though the defendant is not the actual perpetrator. In other words, the information is purely coincidental.

In response to SF's November 13 post, When Justice is as Blind as its Witnesses, the site received an interesting comment pertaining to the charges filed, and later dropped, against Brian Dorian, an off-duty police officer arrested for the homicide of an Illinois man and the shootings of two others. Forensic investigators, using sophisticated digital recovery software, later discovered that Dorian was on his computer on a password accessible Web site at the time of the homicide in Beecher, Illinois.

"Anybody could have been on that computer," wrote the poster, Louis 31. "You're telling me that all I have to do is have someone go on my home computer and access one of my websites requiring a password and I could go on a killing spree? I don't see how your computer being used proves that you were using it. Same truck, same clothes, got new tires the day after, 2nd sketch looks exactly like him, cell phone ping in cedar lake (about 4 miles from where the shooting occurred) from his phone, pulled over in Scherillville IN about 12 miles from the shooting in Indiana, even though he lives in Illinois? Also, the first shooting happened about 2 miles off of Rt. 394 which Brian so happens to live off of."

Before I go further, I am not in possession of any information that corroborates Louis' claims. Hypothetically, however, if these facts are truthful, the "anyone could have been on that computer" statement is somewhat suspect. Encase, the program used to search computers, can see all Web pages accessed and often times determine keystrokes. I believe forensic investigators would attempt to ascertain who had access to the computer and then compare the sites visited and terminology employed by the users. This information is generally compared to previous use in order to show a pattern of password usage and consistency of user(s) verbiage. Furthermore, once in custody, Dorian did not bring the computer to the attention of detectives. This information was retrieved during a later search. Perpetrators attempting to establish alibis are often quick to provide these details to the police.

For Dorian to commit the shooting in Beecher, he would have had to call a person at the computer just prior to the incident and instruct them to log on to the Web site. Of course, had he done so, his cellular and/or residential telephone records would indicate a call was made, which apparently isn't the case.

Moreover, Brian Dorian is a police officer. He likely possesses significant knowledge of the methods used to gather evidence. Why then—during a premeditated attack—would he keep his cellular telephone on to ping off specific towers, and then go on a shooting rampage in a distinguishable vehicle without any attempt to conceal his physical identity? AOL News reports that, after the shooting, police stopped Dorian. He later posted a blurb on his Facebook page stating that officers ordered him from the truck at gunpoint. Why would an off-duty police officer involved in such horrific crimes bring any attention to himself on the Internet?

Time will tell how things shake out. In the interim, I am willing to bet that Louis 31 will keep SF appraised.

POLICE BELIEVE ACTUAL "HONEYBEE SHOOTER" IS 10-7

DECEMBER 14, 2010 | FILED UNDER HOMICIDE

In mid-November, the Spingola Files (SF) posted a story regarding off-duty Lynwood, Illinois Police Officer Brian Dorian, a man initially arrested as the alleged "honeybee shooter." The shootings occurred in the rural community of Beecher, Illinois and also in the border town of Lowell, Indiana, where a farmer was shot by a white male who had stopped to inquire about honeybees.

www.badgerwordsmith.com/spingolafiles/2010/11/13/when-justice-is-as-blind-as-its-witnesses/

After being arrested and charged with one of these horrific crimes, investigators searched Dorian's home computer and learned that he was logged- in to a password accessible Web site at the time of one of the shootings. The Will County DA's office then dropped the charges against Dorian, who professed his innocence.

After the initial post, a comment to this site suggested that SF had gotten it wrong and that the circumstantial evidence strongly pointed to Brian Dorian.

On November 18, SF posted a critique of the Louis 31's comments. I explained that circumstantial evidence might be woven in a way that points to a high probably of guilt, even though a person charged with an offense may be completely innocent.

Many seasoned investigators are aware that circumstantial evidence has been used to convict innocent people of serious crimes. Over the course of the past year, reports abound of persons released from prison due to DNA testing. In these cases, circumstantial evidence was used, in part, to obtain convictions.

As such, SF is not at all surprised that authorities in Illinois now believe that they have identified the actual "honeybee shooter."

On December 11, an armed gunman entered an L.A. Tan salon on South 94th Street in Orland Park, Illinois. While in the process of binding those present, another man—a customer of the salon—entered the store. A confrontation ensued. The customer managed to wrestle a handgun away from the gunman; whereupon, the would-be robber was shot and killed.

Orland Park police identified the now deceased robber as Gary Amaya, 48, of Rankin, Illinois, a small town about 100 miles south of Chicago. Amaya's physical description and his 1992 blue Chevrolet truck are consistent with the perpetrator in the honeybee shooting. Plus, this morning, WBBM radio in Chicago reported that preliminary ballistics testing from the October shootings matched the firearm Amaya used to commit the Orland Park robbery.

Prior to the attempted robbery of the L.A. Tan salon, Amaya tried to handcuff a Chicago prostitute. The woman escaped, although Amaya did fire a shot. Investigators later found her purse inside the suspect's truck.

Arrested and charged with these horrific crimes, authorities have officially cleared Officer Brian Dorian of any wrongdoing.

Hopefully, the skeptics, including Louis 31, as well as those who have already convicted Dorian based on circumstantial evidence—will take a step back and realize that, in certain instances, a series of coincidences are not enough to subject someone to a long prison sentence.

A class act, Brian Dorian is taking things in stride. News reports note that Dorian has kept a low profile until the apprehension of the actual perpetrator. Now, however, he is speaking about his wrongful arrest.

THIS HOLIDAY SEASON, RATS NEEDED

DECEMBER 25, 2010 | FILED UNDER HOMICIDE

It is that time of year, when we gather with family and friends to celebrate Christmas or Hanukkah and, soon, the calendar's entrance into the next decade. To the readers of the Spingola Files (SF), I sincerely hope that you and your families have a blessed and joyous holiday season.

This time of year is often difficult for those whose loved ones are no longer walking among us — due to accident, illness, or homicide.

One such family is the Zimmermanns. A likely would-be burglar took the life of their daughter, Brittany, on April 2, 2008, after a confrontation in the young woman's apartment on Madison's Doty Street.

SF has written about this case in the past, highlighting some of the issues with the initial investigation.

Now, there is some good news to report. It appears that DNA is pointing a finger at a member of a burglary ring. Over the past ten days, several of SF's readers have asked for my take on a Wisconsin State Journal article concerning possible suspects.

While investigators recovered DNA from a window in a July 9, 2008, burglary at Madison's Blue Moon saloon, a search of Wisconsin's database and CODIS, the federal government's national DNA repository, failed to reveal a match. However, Madison police did link three others to the break-in. Twenty-year-old Spencer L. Hutchins and 19-year-olds Darrielle L. Banks and Ryan K. Cook, all of whom made statements admitting their involvement in the incident at the Blue Moon. Authorities now believe that their yet identified accomplice—the fourth person involved in the burglary—is the individual responsible for the Zimmermann homicide.

Fearing reprisal from fellow gang members, Madison detectives are unable to get one of the three to give-up their fellow accomplice. For a brief period in 2009, Hutchins considered an apparent deal for consideration in the burglary sentencing. Citing possible retaliation, he decided against cooperation. The state is now ratcheting-up the pressure by seeking charges of second-degree sexual assault charges against Hutchins for impregnating a 15-year-old girl.

Nonetheless, a handful of SF's readers are curious about the leak of information. The newspaper makes it clear that a family member of one of the individuals that detectives sought to interview called the reporters and supplied the link to the Zimmermann case.

Others have asked why detectives would pass this type of sensitive information along to relatives of possible suspects or witnesses?

While it is simple speculation, I have a hunch that investigators might be trying to heat-up a wire.

Title III of the 1968 Omnibus Crime Control and Safe Streets Act, along with the additional authority contained in the U.S. Patriot Act, enables law enforcement to seek a court order to listen and record landline and cellular telephone calls. Generally, T3s come into play after traditional means of investigation are exhausted.

Obtaining information via a T3 about a specific crime that occurred several years ago is difficult. After two years have passed, the parties involved in these types of conversations could go weeks or months without discussing the incident over the telephone. As a result, investigators need to create a stir by feeding tidbits of information to those with ties to the suspects, believing that these revelations will spark telephone conversations providing needed evidence.

Even though the gang bangers mentioned in the Wisconsin State Journal are unwilling to rat out their accomplice, at the end of the day, their phone conversations over the course of the past two weeks may have done them-in.

If my speculation is correct and detectives are able to develop the identity of a possible suspect in the Zimmermann slaying, the next step is a court ordered DNA sample or obtaining DNA through other investigative means.

Either way, these developments are positive, as the proverbial noose around the neck of Brittany Zimmermann's killer may be slowly tightening.

A PUNISHING STORY OF RUMOR AND INNUENDO

JANUARY 13, 2011 | FILED UNDER COP TALK

McCarthyism—a term coined to describe the tactics of former U.S. Senator Joe McCarthy—is the practice of making allegations of impropriety based primarily on an individual's associations with others, while possessing little or no actual proof of guilt.

History has a way of replicating itself and now it appears that McCarthyism is making a comeback of sorts.

Last Saturday's despicable crimes committed by a psychotic loner in Arizona enabled those with a political agenda—namely Pima County Sheriff Clarence Dupnik—to publicly state that Rush Limbaugh and talk-radio were the catalysts for the tragic shootings of several people. Within a few days, investigators had debunked Dupnik's unprofessional comments, as it became clear that the perpetrator, Jared Loughner, did not listen to talk-radio, watch Fox News, or even read Charles Krauthammer's weekly column in the Washington Post. He is just nuts.

But it was a report in a local newspaper two days prior to the terror in Tucson that highlighted the immergence of a new guilt by association reporters' guild.

In a January 5 article entitled Milwaukee Police Looked into 'Punishers' Group, Milwaukee Journal Sentinel reporter John Diedrich hints that an unnamed police officer is guilty by association. The 'Punishers,' Mr. Diedrich strongly suggests, are a group of rogue Milwaukee police officers.

To back-up his claims, the reporter notes a three-year-old In the Matter Of report filed by Captain James Galezewski, a commander assigned to the training academy. The "arrogant" behavior of a 21-year-old police recruit, Galezewski wrote, as well as a Punisher tattoo on the recruit's upper arm, were cause for termination. In other words, even though this individual had not violated any department rule or state statute, his demeanor was cause for dismissal from the police service.

For the record, Mr. Diedrich does reveal that the officer remains with the Milwaukee Police Department and maintains a clean record of employment.

Milwaukee Police Chief Edward Flynn notes that the Professional Performance Division (PPD), formerly known as Internal Affairs —investigated the existence of the Punishers. PPD determined that the allegations involving this group are simply rumor.

When examining these types of personnel matters, one must consider the size and scope of the Milwaukee Police Department, which has about 2,000 employees. During the course of my career, it was not unusual to see noticeable clicks appear within the ranks. Whether it is a formal organization, such as the Forty Tribunes or the League of Martin, or simply a gathering of friends working at a specific district, subgroups exist within many law enforcement agencies. Associating with others, though, is not violation of MPD policy unless the conduct of the group is inappropriate and/or unlawful.

Having referred to it on several different occasions, Mitchell Nevin's fictional book, The Cozen Protocol, speaks to the issue of subgroups within the Milwaukee Police Department. The novel's elaborate plot focuses on a sinister group of law enforcement veterans entrenched within the department's hierarchy. The book highlights what can occur when miscreant insiders seek to project their influence within a police agency.

While entertaining, The Cozen Protocol's message is that a good conspiracy involves the misdeeds of actual conspirators—speculation and innuendo, premised on tattoos and a cocky demeanor—don't cut it.

FARWELL AVENUE FAIT ACCOMPLI

MAY 8, 2011 | FILED UNDER TRUE CRIME

The late historian William Manchester dubbed his trilogy of Great Britain's legendary leader, Winston Churchill, The Last Lion, in part, because the World War II prime minster was resolute—some would say extremely stubborn—as he roared about extreme political movements on the rise in Europe. Churchill's lion-like tenacity and refusal to fold under pressure made him an iconic political figure – the antithesis of appeasement and eventual capitulation.

From 1964 to 1984, its last lion, Harold A. Breier, led the Milwaukee Police Department. Certainly, as chief-of-police, few, if any, have roared louder or remained as steadfast—rightly or wrongly—in their personal belief system.

While the cataclysmic, Nazi blitzkrieg resulted in Churchill's ascension, it was Breier's resolve to takedown a murderous prison escapee that served as a precursor to his 20-year reign as Milwaukee's most notable and controversial police chief.

On July 4, 1963, Milwaukee was a city of over 800,000, about one-third of which were preparing to cram downtown streets to attend the "Day in Old Milwaukee Circus Parade." This date, however, is best remembered for an event that occurred on the city's lower east side, less than two miles from the parade route.

Just a week earlier, 22-year-old Michael Weston escaped from the Williams Bay correctional camp in Walworth County. A convicted armed robber, Weston somehow traversed 50 miles, undetected, to Milwaukee's south side, where he rented a room above the Tee Pee Inn, located at 1100 S. 1st Street.

In the early morning hours of July 4, Weston was on the lookout for a firearm. He met-up with Ronald Ryan, a 23-year-old south side man, who took $20 from Weston and then traveled with him to 4823 N. 18th Street, the home of Barbara Milligan, a 17-year-old mother of two. Milligan and Weston then went for a stroll in nearby Lincoln Park, where Weston obtained a revolver. Weston then turned the gun on Milligan and demanded $10. Milligan fled the park on foot and ran into a car occupied by Theodore Adams, 19, and his girlfriend, Susan Curro. When he came upon the car, Weston ordered Milligan out, slapped the woman, and threatened to shoot if she did not give him $10. When Adams stepped in between the two, Weston fired two shots, one of which pierced Adams' heart. He died on the scene.

Weston quickly vanished and a massive manhunt ensued. Leading a task force of nearly 100 officers, Detective Inspector Harold Breier scoured the area for the killer. Nearly five hours passed before investigators discovered Weston's hat and coat hidden in a yard two blocks away.

At 11:30 a.m., the owner of the Tee Pee Inn, now aware that a tenant was a wanted fugitive, called to report that Weston had just left the bar. Police soon learned that the killer had taken a cab to the area of S. 17th and W. Mineral Streets, but, by the time officers arrived, Weston was gone.

Then, at about 2:30 p.m., an informant notified detectives that he had observed a man he believed to be Weston walking on Farwell Avenue near E. Brady Street. The informant followed Weston into the East Sider tavern, located at 1677 N. Farwell Avenue, and observed that Weston had a pistol in his lap concealed under a bandana.

In 1963, the Milwaukee Police Department did not have a special weapons and tactics unit. Ballistic vests, similar to those officers wear today, were little more than a pipe dream. Officers were equipped with nothing more than .38 caliber revolvers, handcuffs, callbox keys, and 12-inch nightsticks.

Yet instead of remaining at a command post while members of the task force converged on the target, Breier determined that he, along with Detective Sergeant Edwin Shaffer, take the armed and dangerous Weston into custody.

According to news accounts in the Milwaukee Sentinel, as Breier and Shaffer entered the tavern, the informant gave a signal indicating that Weston was still present. With their revolvers drawn, the officers moved into Weston's view, at which time the killer pointed the gun in Breier's direction. Met by a hail of gunfire, Wetson suffered gunshot wounds to his left arm and chest.

Within a few hours, Weston had confessed to armed robberies at Pat's Tap, 1601 S. 7th Street; the Tuxedo Bar, 2647 N. Downer Street; and the Blue Bar, 1137 W. Maple Street.

To many in Milwaukee, Breier's fearlessness became an overnight legend. Milwaukee Sentinel reporter James G. Wieghart's article entitled Capture Proves Breier's Theory spotlighted the Detective Inspector's mantra: "Don't ask an officer to do anything that you are afraid to do yourself."

A year later, after a national search that included 63 highly qualified candidates, Harold Breier became Milwaukee's chief-of-police.

After tussling with the city's liberal establishment for the next 20 years, Democrats in the state capitol managed to pass Senate Bill 56 (SB-56), also known as the 'Breier Bill,' which limited the scope and authority of the City of Milwaukee's police chief. In 1984, rather than succumb to the edicts from Madison, Breier ended his 44-year career and retired.

But unlike the old soldier of Douglas MacArthur fame, Harold Breier did not simply fade away. In 1984, in an effort to stick a dagger in the eye of Wisconsin Democrats for pushing through SB-56, Breier endorsed incumbent President Ronald Reagan at a rally held at the Bavarian Inn. Ten years later, he led a successful effort to reject a handgun ban in the city of Milwaukee.

Like Winston Churchill—turned away by British voters after the war—critics, such as the members of the Wisconsin Supreme Court, argued that Harold Breier remained in office past his prime, as the demographics and political landscape of Milwaukee changed with the passage of time.

Still, one has to wonder how the history of the Milwaukee Police Department might have changed had Harold Breier did on July 4, 1963, what most high-ranking police officials would do today—remain inside an air conditioned command post while other officers do the things that some do not wish to do themselves.

THE MITCHELL NEVIN ENIGMA

JULY 2, 2011 | COP TALK

Readers of the Spingola Files are keenly aware that I have touted The Cozen Protocol, an alleged fictional book about a Milwaukee gang war and an ensuing police corruption scandal. Well over a year ago now, a young woman from my publishing company called and requested that I review the novel.

Retired Milwaukee Police Department Captain Glenn Frankovis also read The Cozen Protocol and posted a review of the novel at SF:

http://www.badgerwordsmith.com/spingolafiles/2011/02/09/retired-mpd-captain-reviews-milwaukee-based-crime-novel/

About a week after Glenn posted this review, the Milwaukee Small Business Times ran a blurb on their Web site indicating that a group was interested in purchasing the rights to The Cozen Protocol for the purposes of producing a screenplay.

This posting further indicated that Mitchell Nevin is a pen name for the actual author, a Milwaukee law enforcement veteran wishing to remain confidential.

Over the past few months, a handful of active and retired Milwaukee law enforcement officers have inquired as to the author's actual identity. Even though I find it flattering, I can categorically deny that I wrote The Cozen Protocol.

Others have suggested that Glenn Frankovis or active Milwaukee PD Detective John Belsha penned the novel. Both deny having anything to do with the creation of The Cozen Protocol, although I did ask Glenn to review the book for SF.

Of course, I called and conferred with the woman from the publishing company, but she will not "confirm or deny" the identity of the actual author, which has left the matter open to speculation.

As Glenn Frankovis' review of The Cozen Protocol notes, the novel blends fiction with some actual events, one of which is the homicide of a tavern owner killed by an arrow. The incident appears premised on the 1981 death of Karl Lotharius, the former owner of Von Trier's tavern, an east side establishment still open for business on the corner of N. Farwell and E. North Avenues. Just 49-years-old at the time, Lotharius provided the name of his alleged assailant during a dying declaration, but the case went uncharged.

Since The Cozen Protocol seems to provide some significant facts of Lotharius' demise (although, in the book, the victim is Jonathan Donnerstag and the tavern is the Blue Lagoon), some believe the author probably served on the Milwaukee Police Department in the 1970s and 1980s.

I have heard speculation from all corners as to the author's actual identity: a current Milwaukee Police Department assistant chief, a former Milwaukee Police Department assistant chief, a retired homicide detective, and a retired federal agent.

Since the novel paints the police union in a particularly good light, I have my doubts that a high-ranking MPD management-type is the author. John Belsha does seem match two of three criteria of the book's writer: he has significant experience investigating street gangs and serves on the Milwaukee Police Association's Board of Directors. John, however, adamantly denies having anything to do with The Cozen Protocol.

Moreover, whoever wrote the book has experience working death investigation scenes, as the dialog between characters is strikingly familiar to the real world. One example is a homicide at Pedro the Peruvian Barber's shop, where a masked man shoots and kills a Latino gang leader. For those who worked Milwaukee's south side in the 1980s and 1990s, the locale is a likely spoof of Tony the Columbian Barber's shop, on Chavez Drive (formerly S. 16th Street), near South Division High School. The conversation between the sergeant, a detective, the medical examiner and an officer is uniquely Milwaukee.

Rumors abound that some media-types are in the process of tracking down the actual author. This writing probably saved those investigating a little extra legwork.

WHEN BIG BROTHER REACHES OUT AND TOUCHES

SEPTEMBER 24, 2011 | CITIZEN TALK

A recent Wall Street Journal technology article serves-up yet another chilling reminder that America's national security infrastructure is gobbling-up the privacy of the citizens it is suppose to serve and protect.

Since the events of September 11, 2001, the federal government has spent around $500 billion developing a nationwide domestic intelligence network. The "about $500 billion" is an estimate because the total cost of secret domestic monitoring operations is unknown, even to many federally elected officials and former high-ranking intelligence agency bureaucrats.

Currently, 74 fusion centers dot the nation's landscape, with each state having at least one. Wisconsin has two active fusion centers—one in Madison, operated by the Wisconsin Department of Justice, and another in Milwaukee, run by the Milwaukee Police Department.

Proponents of fusion centers—primarily state and federal law enforcement officials—will claim—with a straight face—that the purpose of these intelligence centers is fighting the war on terror. However, with cheesehead Islamic terrorists few-and-far between, the missions of these federally subsidized outfits was expanded to include criminal and even non-criminal activity. In plain English, the activities of American citizens, not just terrorists, are now fair game.

Critics of these taxpayer funded data collection units believe fusion centers serve as a front for domestic spy operations. In the past, Suspicious Incident Report (SAR) forms, filed by law enforcement officers, have listed a handful of Catholic nuns as terror threats. At least one supporter of presidential candidate Ron Paul alleges that a fusion center report identified her as a possible security risk.

Last Thursday, Wall Street Journal technology reporter Jennifer Valentino-Devries took an in-depth look at one high profile case that pits fusion center technology against the U.S. Constitution's Fourth Amendment.

The article details the use of "Stingray" electronic ease dropping equipment used by fusion center operatives to locate and obtain intelligence from the cellular telephones of American citizens. This technology, sold to the public as necessary to fight the war on terror, was used to nab Daniel David Rigmaiden, an American citizen and simple computer hacker.

Under the U.S. Supreme Court guidelines established in Brady v. Maryland, the government is obligated to provide Rigmaiden full and absolute discovery of all reports, as well as other relevant information obtained by investigators.

Since the late 1950s, American courts have viewed virtually all civilian criminal prosecutions as transparent examinations of the state's evidence. This public process is what separates American jurisprudence from that of totalitarian nations, like China, Iran, and, to a lesser extent, Russia.

Even though federal agents had no qualms using top-secret StingRay technology to get their man, federal prosecutors are now refusing to disclose how the technology operates. The defense, of course, needs to examine the use of the cellular telephone signal interceptor in order to see if it correctly identified Rigmaiden; thereby, creating a quandary for the prosecution. If the federal government refuses to comply with Rigmaiden's discovery request, a federal district court judge in Arizona might grant the defense's motion to dismiss the case.

In open court, the Rigmaiden case is shedding light on the cost and the scope of Big Brother—the domestic spy apparatus developed since 9/11. Even though the Congressional Budget Office and Obama administration officials project trillion dollar annual deficits until 2019, money is not a problem when it comes to conducting surveillance of Americans absent a reasonable suspicion. At a cost of $3.4 billion, the Department of Homeland Security's new complex will rival the Pentagon in size. If one wonder's why it costs between $83 to $120 billion annually just to operate and staff 74 intelligence fusion centers, take a look at the number of cameras deployed outside home improvement stores, on the tops of poles at busy thoroughfares, and along interstate highways. DHS has also installed chemical sensors and X-ray machines at truck stops and at other key interstate highway locations.

With the federal debut set to increase nearly 60 percent from 2009 through 2012, rumors have it that Department of Homeland Security Secretary Janet Napolitano, a.k.a. Big Sis, has pulled the federally funding for Milwaukee's fusion center. Can Police Chief Edward Flynn, Mayor Barrett, and fusion center operatives come-up with the estimated $12.9 million to fund Milwaukee's domestic surveillance initiative? My guess is they will, even if police response times suffer at the expense of staffing the fusion center 24 x 7, 365 days a year.

In the interim, who is providing the necessary oversight of these centers as they compile data on every day Americans? I guess we will never know, since it is all top secret.

BEATING BACK THE 'BUSH'

NOVEMBER 26, 2011 | FILED UNDER ORGANIZED CRIME

Since mid-1960s, Madison, Wisconsin, has maintained a reputation as one of the nation's popular college towns. During the Vietnam War, campus radicals from Wisconsin's flagship university held sit-ins, challenged the police, and bombed a campus physics building. One of those campus radicals, Paul Soglin, has served several stints—including one currently ongoing—as Madison's mayor.

In the first half of the 20th Century, groups loosely affiliated with La Cosa Nostra outfits in Chicago dominated the news in Madison. Immigrants from Sicily, as well as their second-generation families, flooded Greenbush, a cluster of neighborhoods on that city's near south side, known to locals as the 'Bush.'

Like other immigrant communities throughout the United States, Madison's Sicilian section of town quickly developed a reputation as a tough place to do business. When violence erupted, the police generally shook the 'Bush' for suspects.

The first in a series of infamous crimes in 'the Bush' occurred in the early morning of February 4, 1918. Coming home from working the graveyard shift in Madison's Shank's corner's neighborhood, 30-year-old off-duty patrolman Grant Dosch passed-by the Louis Cohen General Merchandise Store, located at 754 W. Washington Ave. Investigators believe Dosch observed more than one person inside the store, as the perpetrators used a chisel to force a door on the south side of the building. The crime scene suggests that a lookout man stationed across the street fired two shotgun blasts. One shattered Dosch's jawbone with the other struck Dosch above his right eye.

Groans from the ailing officer awoke Elmer Currie, who went outside investigate. Currie found Dosch lying on the sidewalk with a revolver at his side. Medical personnel rushed Dosch to St. Mary's hospital, but the off-duty officer later succumbed to wounds.

At the scene, detectives located a loaded doubled-barreled shotgun directly across the street from Louis Cohen's store. Seeking to gain the confidence of Greenbush residence, The Capital Times reported that Madison police enlisted the help of "an Italian detective assigned to the Beloit police force."

Investigators later arrested three suspects: John and Tony Mazzaro, and Peter Messina, all of whom were later charged. Thirteen months after the Dosch's murder, a sensational trial ensued, which resulted in the acquittal of the three men.

The death of Patrolman Dosch, and the subsequent acquittal of the three suspects, bolstered the 'Bush's' tough-as-nails reputation. Police officials, journalists, and city residents soon tagged sections of Greenbush with mob-type monikers. 'Death's corner,' the area surrounding Murray Street and Desmond Court, earned its reputation as a murderer's row.

On a hot August evening in 1922, James D'Amico, a.k.a. Jimmy the Limp, was gun-downed on the steps of a store at 16 Murray Street (in contemporary Madison, the location is approximately eight blocks northeast of the Kohl Center). On the run from the Chicago outfit for a half-decade, some believed rivals followed D'Amico back to Madison after he secretly attended a relative's funeral in Chicago.

Then on December 1, 1924, an anonymous telephone call alerted police that one of their own, Patrolman Herbert Dreger, was lying on the ground in a pool of blood in the 100 block of Murray Street. Rushed to the hospital, Dreger's last words were, "Those guys in the god damn lunch got me." Investigators later apprehended San Dimartino, who was in possession one-half of a shotgun. Two days later, the other half of the firearm was located in a nearby yard. Detectives determined that the two pieces were an exact fit. Also arrested was Frank Vitalle, who, according to the United Press, "attempted to pull a gun on the officers arresting him, but was subdued by a blow to the jaw."

Because of pre-trial publicity (and probably in part to the prosecution's belief that a jury consisting of at least one intimidated Sicilian may not convict), the trial was moved to Baraboo, Wisconsin, where a jury once again acquitted both men.

Over the course of time, City of Madison planners have deliberately demolished the old Greenbush neighborhood. With these streets and neighborhoods virtually wiped from the map, remnants of the 'Bush' are few-and-far between—typically found only in the names of a handful of businesses that occasionally sprout-up in what was the former home of little Italy.

Today, Madison's high profile homicides no longer involve Italian gangsters and police officers. Instead, the victims are college co-eds, such as Brittany Zimmermann and Kelly Nolan. Even though the 'Bush' no longer exists, some things never really change, as justice for these two women is—as was the case with patrol officers Dosch and Dreger— proving illusive.

DEADPAN DRIFTER

MAY 14, 2010 AT 2:06 PM | FILED UNDER HOMICIDE

As a young boy, Edward Edwards spent time in a Catholic orphanage. When a nun caught him stealing birthday cake, she asked the troubled child what he envisioned himself doing as an adult. "I looked her straight in the eyes and answered, ' Sister, I'm gonna be a crook, and I'm gonna be a good one," Edwards wrote in his book, Metamorphosis of a Criminal.

No doubt, Edwards' led the life of a crook, although a bad one. He spent his early adult years hitchhiking across the country, robbing gas stations, and writing bad checks. During the robberies, he did not use a mask, which made him easily identifiable.

From the mid-1950s to the late 1960s, Edwards was incarcerated in various locations throughout the country. Released from a federal prison in Lewisburg, Pennsylvania in 1967, he developed a new con — that of the reformed career criminal. In 1972, he published his memoir, Metamorphosis of a Criminal. The book's title rang true, as Edwards evolved from a two-bit robbery suspect in to a cold-blooded killer.

Edwards' childhood development pointed to signs of a troubling life as an adult.

In his book, Journey into Darkness, retired FBI criminal profiler John Douglas notes that, at a very young age, many serial killers develop behaviors that are part of the "homicidal triad." These include bed-wetting at an inappropriate age, starting fires, and cruelty to animals. Futuristic killers typically emanate from broken homes, and, in general, are in some way abused as children — either physically, sexually or emotionally. "Throughout their lives," Douglas writes, "they [serial killers] believe they've been victims: they've been manipulated, they've been dominated, they've been controlled by others."

By his own admission, Edwards suffered from enuresis and experienced physical abuse while growing-up at the orphanage.

After his con as a reformed career criminal received scant attention, Edwards faded into obscurity and drifted throughout the country. In 1980, he found employment as a maintenance man at the Concord House, in the small, spit-and-miss-it town of the same namesake, located about 43 miles west of Milwaukee in eastern Jefferson County, Wisconsin.

On August 10, a young couple, Timothy Hack and Kelly Drew, disappeared after attending a wedding reception at the Concord House. Initially, family members thought that the couple might have eloped, although the evidence dictated otherwise. Hack's car remained parked outside the dance hall, where his wallet and checkbook were located. The two families recruited hundreds of searchers and a small reward fund was established. Investigators later found Drew's purse and its contents dumped along a road between Concord and the sleepy town of Farmington.

On October 19, two hunters stumbled upon a nude corpse located near the town of Ixonia, about five-and-a-half miles north of the Concord House. Detectives quickly identified the body of Kelly Drew. After an intense search of the area, state agents discovered Hack's corpse in a nearby cornfield. Having sat in an open field for two months, the bodies of the couple decomposed to the point where forensic pathologists had a difficult time discerning the actual cause of death.

The case took a strange twist when a controversial private investigator, Norbert Kutczewski, purported that a satanic cult had a hand in the slayings. The Jefferson County Sheriff ripped this theory. Mother time would later prove the sheriff correct. And, of course, like many other unsolved homicides at the time, investigators included the name of another drifter, Henry Lucas. Still, the case ran cold for nearly 27 years.

In 2007, investigators submitted cold case DNA — semen discovered on the Drew's clothing — for testing. Crime lab analysts forwarded the results to CODIS, the FBI's national DNA data bank. Nearly a year-and-a-half later, a positive hit came back to Edwards, who was living quietly in a Louisville, Kentucky trailer park.

Investigators had interviewed Edwards shortly after the couple's disappearance. However, he left the area in September 1980 and later popped-up in Pennsylvania, where he torched a house he had been renting — fulfilling the second prong of John Douglas' "homicidal triad."

After serving his sentence for arson, Edwards' whereabouts in the 1990s are unclear. Investigators do know that resided in the Louisville trailer park since 2001. At the time of his arrest, he was married.

Suspecting Edwards might be involved in other murders or even a serial killer; investigators searched the FBI's Violent Criminal Apprehension Program (ViCAP) database, but could not positively link Edwards to other homicides.

Jefferson County and state investigators carefully sifted through Edwards' background and travel history in an attempt to ascertain his whereabouts on June 7, 1974, the day 17-year-old Oconomowoc High School senior Catherine Sjoberg disappeared after attending her prom at the Concord House. Sjoberg had a significant disagreement with her prom date and walked out of the dance, leaving him behind. Her body has yet to be located. Considered the prime suspect in her disappearance, detectives grilled her prom date, although he later passed three subsequent polygraph examinations.

Earlier this month, the Milwaukee Journal Sentinel reported that Edwards, now 76, had written a letter to prosecutors in Ohio on April 9 requesting an interview with detectives regarding two 1977 homicides. In this letter, Edwards noted that he was aging, in poor health, and that investigators may want to "stick a needle" in his arm after the interview. Reports have surfaced that Edwards confessed to murdering a young couple, William Lavaco, 21, of Doylestown, Ohio, and Judith Straub, 18, of Sterling, Ohio, who were found dead from gunshot wounds in a city park.

One can only theorize why Edwards is coming forward with this information, although his trial was once again delayed. Suffering from a slew of health problems, the obese Edwards requires a wheel chair for courtroom appearances. Without a doubt, investigators from various parts of the country will likely spend some time with the dying Edwards while there is still some left.

PROWLERS ON THE PARKWAY: SF'S TAKE ON THE COLONIAL PARKWAY MURDERS

JUNE 11, 2010 AT 2:57 AM | FILED UNDER HOMICIDE

From June 3 – 7, the Spingola Files (SF) visited Virginia to explore the murders of six people and the disappearances of two others near the Colonial Parkway. SF examined the crime scenes, spoke to those familiar with the investigations, listened to tipsters, and spoke to family members of the victims. After careful thought, SF believes these homicides are probably not directly related.

Consider the following set of facts:

On October 12, 1986, a passing jogger noticed a white Honda resting on an embankment just off the Colonial Parkway. National Park Service rangers, believing the car was in an accident, shattered the windows, only to discover the bodies of Cathy Thomas and Rebecca Dowski— both of whom had their throats badly slit. The violent attack almost decapitated Ms. Thomas. The crime scene on the Colonial Parkway embankment strongly suggests the slayings occurred outside the vehicle. The assailant then placed both bodies inside the Honda while attempting to destroy telling evidence with diesel fuel. When the liquid failed to ignite, the suspect dumped the Honda on the nearby embankment.

In the Thomas/Dowski case the suspect used ligatures to control the victims, while, I believe, cutting their throats from behind. In this case, I've developed the following profile of the perpetrator: a white or Asian male, possibly an authority figure, with a working knowledge of edged weapons, knot typing, and boating. This individual probably has a military or para-military background.

I do not see a direct link between the Thomas/Dowski homicides and other Colonial Parkway murders; however, the modus operandi is very similar to the slayings of Julie Williams and Lollie Winans, which occurred in the Shenandoah National Park around May 27, 1996. Both of these alternative lifestyle couples died either inside or near national parks and had their throats slit in a manner that is eerily familiar.

During the Shenandoah visit, information gleaned from various sources enabled SF to locate the probable Williams/Winans crime scene — a location much closer to the Skyland Lodge that previously advertised. Like the Thomas/

Dowski homicides, the killer probably observed the couple for a time prior to the slayings. From my experience in criminal investigative analysis, I believe that the killer is an individual with a strong distain for lesbians. Based on the level of brutality, these two cases have the markings of significant acts of hate.

Nonetheless, the other Colonial Parkway crimes have different signatures.

On September 19/20, 1987, David Knobling, 20, and Robin Edwards, 14, were the next couple found murdered. These homicides did not occur in or around the Colonial Parkway, but inside the Ragged Island Wildlife Refuge in Isle of Wright County — on the other side of a long bridge from York County. Law enforcement initially located Knobling's Ford Ranger truck in a parking lot about a football field from where the bodies of the couple washed ashore. Both suffered fatal gunshot wounds to the back of the head, suggesting execution-style killings. I have no doubt that the slayings of Knobling and Edwards occurred at this location.

Furthermore, a review of the Ragged Island crime scene suggests two distinct possibilities: a robbery or a small-time drug-rip gone badly. First off, Knobling's Ford Ranger was parked feet from a major arterial highway. My impression of the area that it is not a serial killer's stomping ground; however, my gut tells me it is a good spot to meet for a quick exchange of product for cash.

On the other hand, the April 10, 1988 disappearance of Keith Call and Cassandra Hailey remains an enigma. Without bodies, it is difficult to ascertain a motive. Keith and Cassandra went on their first date that night. Instead of attending a movie as planned, the couple stopped by a party that took place in the University Square area. The building where the party occurred no longer exists, as several older structures in this area — about 15 miles from the Colonial Parkway — were torn down and brick buildings erected in their place several years ago. The couple left the gathering together, in the early morning. Investigators later found Call's 1982 Toyota abandoned on the Colonial Parkway, about a one-half mile from the location of the Thomas/Dowski homicides.

To surmise what may or may not have occurred, an examination of Call's vehicle is in order. Personally, I believe the suspects strategically placed the vehicle on the Colonial Parkway. I used the word "suspects" because more than one person was involved. Keith Call wasn't the last person to operate his Toyota on the morning he met his fate. One perpetrator transported the vehicle to the Colonial Parkway; whereby, he or she was then picked-up by the co-conspirator(s).

This leaves the last known murder victims, Daniel Lauer, 21, and Annamaria Phelps, 18.

Law enforcement discovered Lauer's 1973 Chevrolet Nova parked in the acceleration lane of an I-64 New Kent County east bound rest stop with the keys in the ignition and the gas tank three-quarters full. Investigators determined the car to be in working condition, although they found red dirt and weeds trapped in the undercarriage. Six weeks later, bow hunters located the badly decomposed remains of Lauer and Phelps just seven-tenths of a mile from the rest stop. The crime scene is at the end of a logging trail, located adjacent to Courthouse Road, which is the first exit off I-64 after leaving the rest stop.

While looking at the Lauer/Phelps case, it is important to note that, back in the 1980s, New Kent County was a sleepy place in no hurry to catch-up to American civilization. One source told us that during the time frame of the Lauer/Phelps homicides, deputies in New Kent County often used their personal vehicles for official business. Until this day, New Kent does not have its own county jail. As such, it doesn't take a stretch of one's imagination to envision the level of investigative resources available for mobilization. After all, even Mayberry — the small-town inhabited by Opie, Otis, and Barney Fyfe — had a jail. A lack of resources and investigative wherewithal may explain how a sheriff's department with two missing adults would fail to thoroughly search the area within a square mile of the abandoned vehicle. Had the New Kent County Sheriff's Department and the Virginia State Police done so, they might have uncovered valuable evidence at the crime scene destroyed by weather, animals, and decomposition.

After looking at the scene and speaking to sources in the area, my hunch is the Lauer/Phelps homicides were the handiwork of a police impersonator. True, the Phelps family finds it odd that investigators located the car abandoned in the eastbound side of the rest stop while they believe the couple was last traveling westbound. However, if the couple, for some reason, either missed the westbound rest stop area or had a change of heart about stopping, they would then exit I-64 westbound, pass over a bridge, and reenter I-64 east, where the rest stop is located. Why not use the first rest stop, which is on the east bound side?

As far as suspects, I believe the Lauer/Phelps homicides are two that probably merited relatively quick resolutions. The use of the nearby logging trail is an indication that the perpetrator is clearly someone with knowledge of the area. He feels comfortable in New Kent County, knows the haunts of the area, as well as the back roads. I would be surprised if this was the first significant crime he committed, although with the lack of resources applied to law enforcement by the 1980s New Kent political establishment — the killer may have fallen between the cracks.

On another note, as the Colonial Parkway cases are concerned, the New Kent County Sheriff's Department wasn't the only law enforcement agency to drop the ball. The Isle of Wright PD lost a set of fingerprints. Other sets of fingerprints sat for decades without a search through the FBI's national data base. One victim managed to grab a hold of the suspect's hair, although it appears the hair sat in an evidence locker since its recovery absent DNA or any other type of analysis. Granted, members of every law enforcement agency in the US make mistakes. Yet an agency's willingness to step-up to the plate and admit culpability while, at the same time, dedicating the resources to right the wrong, separates law enforcement professionals from political hacks trying to cover their back ends.

PSYCHOLOGY OF HOMICIDE PRESENTATION NOW AVAILABLE NATIONALLY

JUNE 19, 2010 AT 6:34 PM | FILED UNDER TRUE CRIME

Over the course of the past two years, I have been very fortunate to speak to small groups, members of the press, and others regarding the profiles and backgrounds of homicide suspects. The feedback received from Spingola Files' events is overwhelmingly positive. One person recently told me she felt as if the presentation itself was a live version of the hit television show Criminal Minds.

If you are a member of a group or organization in need of a guest speaker, please consider the Spingola Files' presentation, The Psychology of Homicide—an entertaining hour-and-a-half speaking engagement featuring yours truly.

Having spent almost 15 years working homicides in various capacities, I use a Power Point presentation to walk those in attendance through challenging crime scenes, discuss motives and opportunities, and then explore the backgrounds of various suspects.

Some of the cases include Jeffrey Dahmer, the North Side Strangler homicides, the unsolved case of a 15-year-old newspaper delivery boy killed by an improvised explosive device, and the mysterious disappearance of a young Milwaukee girl.

DECADES-OLD COLD CASES FOCUS ON IMPROVED DNA TESTING

JULY 18, 2010 AT 5:00 PM | FILED UNDER HOMICIDE

Almost 20-years-ago to the day, Berit Beck, 18, went missing while en route from her Sturtevant, Wisconsin home to a computer-training course in Appleton. Investigators later located the attractive young woman's van in a Fond du Lac K-Mart parking lot—a city of 42,000 forty-three miles south of Beck's destination.

Since Beck hoped to recoup the expenses associated with the costs of travel, prior to leaving, she jotted down the van's miles. The odometer indicated that the vehicle logged 597 miles, 462 miles more than needed to reach Appleton.

Law enforcement launched an extensive search, but almost six weeks passed before Beck's body was located in ditch near the city of Waupun—just over 18 miles to the east of the van's recovery.

An autopsy concluded that Beck died of probable strangulation, although decomposition resulted in the probable loss of valuable physical evidence.

While the murder of Berit Beck remains unsolved, just two days ago—on the 20th anniversary of her disappearance—investigators from the Fond du Lac County Sheriff's Department resubmitted DNA recovered from the van and Beck's corpse.

Resubmitting DNA evidence is common practice in cold case homicide investigations. As the techniques used to test DNA advance, labs can now analyze smaller samples. Moreover, as time passes, state and federal DNA databases continue to expand, increasing the chances of a positive hit.

A prime example is the homicide of 19-year-old Kathleen Leichtman.

On July 14, 1976, Leichtman left Milwaukee to work as an exotic dancer at The Other Place—a strip club near Fond du Lac. Later that evening, she left the club in the company of two men. At 2 a.m. on July 15, a motorist observed Leichtman's body lying near a golf course road, with her throat slit. She also suffered other multiple stab wounds. The investigation turned cold for nearly 33-years.

In 2001, investigators submitted DNA recovered from the Leichtman crime scene but failed to receive a positive hit. Then in September 2008, authorities resubmitted the DNA, which matched Thomas Niesen, a 53-year-old Green Bay man. Earlier that year, a court convicted Niesen of felony child abuse.

Wisconsin law compels convicted felons to provide DNA samples.

A photo of Niesen from 1976 virtually matched a composite sketch of one of the men observed leaving The Other Place with Leichtman.

Neisen married shortly after the slaying. He later told his now ex-wife, Ja Cee Crull, that the last time he had visited The Other Place things went "horribly" wrong and he ended-up killing a woman. Crull, however, refused to come forward with this information until approached by detectives three-decades after the fact.

In the Berit Beck investigation, the Fond du Lac County Sheriff's Department is hoping that lightning strikes twice and that enhanced DNA testing results in a hit with CODIS—the FBI's national DNA database. However, if these resubmissions test negative, a probably exists that the perpetrator in Beck's murder is likely deceased.

Theories concerning the slaying of Berit Beck abound.

Last May, Chris Martin, a minister turned author, published Urges: a Chronicle of Serial Killer Larry Hall. Martin alleges that Hall might be responsible for the slayings of Beck and another Wisconsin woman, Laurie Depies.

However, when pressed for more information linking Hall to the homicides of Beck and Depies, the author seems to premise his allegations solely on geography.

"The very fact that you have two murders in proximity," is how Martin justified his theory connecting Hall to WTMJ television's Charles Benson.

That's a flimsy hypothesis, which, if used as loosely by law enforcement, could brand hundreds of otherwise innocent people as serial killers.

In fact, the likelihood of Hall being Beck's killer is slim considering that Hall's DNA is on file with CODIS and earlier testing from the Beck case failed to return a positive hit. Furthermore, from what I've read about Larry Hall, some of his claims appear, at best, dubious; this is why DNA evidence is particularly valuable.

WAS COMMUNICATION IN SERIAL STABBING CASE LACKING?

AUGUST 17, 2010 AT 4:01 PM | FILED UNDER HOMICIDE

The arrest of alleged serial killer Elias Abuelazam has apparently resulted in some finger pointing. An August 17, 2010, article in USA Today, entitled Networking Helps ID Serial Attacks, claims police in Flint, Michigan "did not begin discussing the possibility of a serial killer until late July, when the area had six stabbings over six straight nights."

Authorities in Michigan believe Abuelazam is a probable serial killer who operated in at least three states—Michigan, Ohio, and Virginia. The killer's modus operandi: use the pretext of car trouble to ask for assistance from minority citizens and then stab the Good Samaritan helpers.

In the USA Today article, Steven Egger, a University of Houston—Clear Lake Criminology professor, claims the lack of communication among local police departments is a national problem. "Police officers," Egger states, "are not trained to network."

I disagree.

For years now, the FBI has operated the ViCAP program—an initiative available to virtually every law enforcement agency throughout the United States. ViCAP categorizes the homicides that occur throughout the country for the purpose of assisting local law enforcement.

Of course, ViCAP is only as good as the information provided by police departments. If an agency withholds or fails to disclose ViCAP data, law enforcement agencies searching for homicides with similar MOs will come-up empty handed.

Which leads one to wonder: did USA Today reporter Alan Gomez miss an opportunity to commit a flagrant act of investigative journalism by simply asking Flint PD officials when the data from the six stabbings in their jurisdiction was entered into ViCAP?

For whatever reasons, local law enforcement officials are sometimes hesitant to provide information regarding serious crimes to other agencies. When this occurs, the typical response from the bureaucracy centers around 'the need to know.'

But, as the Abuelazm case illustrates, the FBI—through ViCAP—as well as other law enforcement agencies NEED TO KNOW about homicides in other jurisdictions.

Certainly, USA Today would do its readers a service by asking some tough questions from Flint officials instead of finding a professor—one who may have few, if any, law enforcement credentials—to provide unknowing-cover for the 'need to know' insiders.

On another note, while I generally refuse to publicly speculate about major crimes absent first-hand information, many readers have asked what I believe is Abuelazam's motive. It's only a hunch, but an educated guess is that, at one point in time, Abuelazam's car may have broken down at which time he was robbed. His attacks may be a continuous act of retaliation.

THE FALLS GUY: PART I

AUGUST 1, 2010 AT 3:27 PM | FILED UNDER HOMICIDE

Under the leadership of Police Chief Edward Flynn, Milwaukee has seen its crime numbers drop for ten consecutive quarters. Last Thursday, the Milwaukee Police Department reported that violent crime had decreased 30.8 percent since 2007. Last year, Milwaukee recorded 72 homicides, the lowest total since 1985.

But things were much different in the fall of 1990 when Milwaukee's per capita homicide rate boosted the city to eighth in the murder capitol of the world rankings. Like other major American urban areas, Milwaukee was in the midst of a major crack cocaine epidemic. The increase in homicides—up about 47 percent from 1985 to 1990—strained the resources of the Milwaukee Police Department.

The early evening hours of Friday, November 2, 1990, told the tale of a city losing its grip to drugs and a propensity for violence. The unseasonably warm 70-degree temperature caused many to partake in one last gasp of summer before the onslaught of Wisconsin's harsh winter.

At District Five, officers taking-in early shift roll call—the few in blue preparing to hit the streets from 4 p.m. to 12 midnight—had no idea how intense and long their purported eight hour tour of duty would soon become.

During rush hour, two squads were dispatched to 11th and Locust for a vehicular homicide—known, back in the day, as a 20-pointer, for the twenty questions officers were required to answer for such investigations. A motorcycle driven by a 35-year-old Milwaukee man struck a curb sending the 25-year-old passenger airborne into a city light pole. Even though the passenger barely suffered a bruise, the crushing blow severed his aorta. Death was virtually instantaneous.

An hour later, other District Five units were sent to the scene of what would be yet another homicide.

By 11 p.m., the north side was so a buzz with activity that a dispatcher found just enough time between transmissions to relay a message that the early shift was "extended until further notice."

It was, however, a call given to early shift officers—still on overtime the following morning at 2:52 a.m.—that typified the troubles of a city at the zenith of a crime wave. A dispatcher directed officers to a home at 3021 N. 8th

Street for a report double homicide.

At the time, the area of N. Eighth and W. Burleigh Streets was one of Milwaukee's troubled spots. Just three blocks away, the corner of Ninth Street and Concordia Ave. supported a well-known open-air drug distribution network.

Milwaukeeans growing-up in the 1950s, such as Milwaukee Brewers play-by-play announcer Bob Uecker, nostalgically refer to this location as the old Borchert Field neighborhood, the home of the American Association Milwaukee Brewers from 1902 to 1952. The stadium, reminiscent of the old polo grounds in New York, was leveled in 1953 and currently services six lanes of I-43 traffic, which abuts Eighth Street directly to the east.

When officers arrived at 3021 N. 8th Street, they found a distraught 33-year-old mother, Karen Scott, at the front door. Just minutes before, Scott returned home to find two of her daughters, Latrice Scott, 7, and Monika Scott, 11, with their throats slit. Scott's other daughter, 11-month-old Jeanette, was found lying on a sofa with a baby bottle.

Clad in a pink outfit, Latrice Scott was found face down in a pool of blood facing west in a first-floor bedroom. Officers discovered Monika Scott face-up in a pantry adjacent to a dining area with her throat noticeably slit. She was naked from the waist down.

On the porch outside her home, Karen Scott initially explained that she had left her daughters in the company of her boyfriend, John A. Falls, who was noticeably absent.

Investigators had a solid suspect for the grisly crime—an apparent sexual homicide and the killing of a young witness.

As homicide detectives arrived to process the scene, Karen Scott, in the company of an officer, went to a neighbor's home a few doors down the street. Once there, she later told the officer that she had left her children alone and that Falls was not present, although she suspected he could have easily persuaded Monika to allow him inside the home.

Falls, who had no criminal record, became the target of a short manhunt. He was located at his mother's home and later arrested.

But what version of events were investigators to believe? Did Karen Scott leave her children with her boyfriend and change her story to provide cover for him or did she actually leave her 11-year-old daughter in charge?

NEXT: the Falls Guy and Physical Evidence

THE FALLS GUY: PART II

AUGUST 14, 2010 AT 12:33 PM | FILED UNDER HOMICIDE

In the early morning hours of November 3, 1990, just a few houses south of a vicious crime scene on N. Eighth Street, Karen Scott—the mother of two murder victims, Latrice Scott, 7, and Monika Scott, 11—sat in the living room of a neighbor's home in the company of a Milwaukee police officer. Karen Scott initially told investigators that she had left her children with her boyfriend. Over the course of the next two hours, however, her version of events began to change.

According to Karen Scott, her boyfriend at the time, John Falls, was "crazy drunk" and the two had fought for most of the previous day. Falls later left the house, as did Karen, who left 11-year-old Monika in-charge. Even though her boyfriend did not have a key to the residence, Karen believed Falls, in a drunken stupor, might have forced his way into the basement and then talked his way inside.

Detectives later located Falls at his mother's home recovering from a hard-drinking bender, where he was placed under arrest, conveyed to the detective bureau, and interrogated for almost 28 hours. He confessed to the homicides of the two young girls, even though he was so intoxicated that he had suffered a significant blackout.

As Falls wallowed away in the county jail awaiting trial for the next nine months, the man with no criminal record believed detective's had convinced him that he committed the homicides, even though—due to the alcohol induced blackout—he had no actual recollection of events.

Represented by one of the better attorney's in the Wisconsin Public Defender's office, Falls requested further forensic testing of the physical evidence. While DNA evidence, at the time, was in its infancy, technicians at the Wisconsin Regional Crime Lab determined that hairs recovered from Monika Scott's pubic mound did not belong to John Falls.

Falls also retracted his confession made under the duress of lengthily questioning, although a Milwaukee County judge denied his motion to suppress his statements to detectives.

The state's case against Falls could have proceeded, but, believing Falls may not be the actual killer, the Milwaukee County District Attorney's office withdrew the criminal complaint. A judge later released Falls from custody.

But the question remained: who killed the two young girls?

Early in 2008, the Milwaukee Police Department established a cold case unit. One of the first investigations the two detectives, Gilbert Hernandez and Kathy Hein, explored was the grizzly scene on N. Eighth Street. Ironically, Hernandez—working early shift patrol out of District Five—was one of the officers on the scene that morning.

"I remember them [the scene detectives] saying," Hernandez told the Milwaukee Journal Sentinel, in reference to the vicious slayings, "'You do not want to go in there.'"

Unfortunately, over two years have passed and, so far, an identifiable DNA match has proven elusive. It is possible the perpetrator's DNA is not in the state's database. On the other hand, the lack of a DNA match could also imply that the killer himself is no longer with us. Those who live by the sword often die by it. Karma—as in what goes around, comes around—is sometimes the vehicle of justice doled-out to those living by the no-holds barred rules of the mean streets of Milwaukee.

A CRY FROM THE GRAVE

DECEMBER 12, 2010 AT 5:43 PM | FILED UNDER HOMICIDE

The mantra within the Milwaukee Police Department's Homicide Unit is that detectives investigating the final moments of a victim's life speak for those no longer with a voice. The origins of this particular saying emanate from the world's first murder, when Cain stabbed and killed his brother Abel, documented, as follows, in the fourth chapter of Genesis, versus one through three:

The Lord said to Cain, "Where is your brother, Abel?"

"I know not," Cain replied. "Am I my brother's keeper?"

Then the Lord said, "What have you done? Your brother's blood cries out to me from the ground."

Unlike the almighty, however, homicide detectives cannot literally hear a victim calling from the grave. And, unfortunately, sometimes the cries of those meeting a violent death never get a hearing.

One such person whose blood has cried out from a muddy river bank for over 41 years with little response is Stephanie Casberg.

An attractive, recent graduate of Milwaukee's Riverside High School, Casberg was just a week shy of her 18th birthday when she left her part-time job and was never seen alive again. A few sketchy details pertaining to Casberg's tragic death are featured on the Milwaukee Police Department's cold case Web page. To fill-in some gaps, SF researched the matter with the hopes of dislodging the cobwebs from someone's long-term memory.

In July 1969, Milwaukee was much different place. Young, draft eligible protestors staged sit-ins and racial tensions ran high, although city leaders had high hopes for a new music festival, Summerfest—now a nationally recognized entertainment venue—that was readying for its July 18 – 27 ten-day run. And downtown Milwaukee, especially the area east of the Milwaukee River, was in the very early stages of what is now a bustling revitalization.

Built in 1965 with the hopes of encouraging professionals to reside downtown, the 27-story Juneau Village Tower apartments had spurred the construction of a cluster of shops in the 1100 block on N. Van Buren Street.

One such tenant of this new development was the now defunct Marc's Big Boy restaurant, where Stephanie Casberg waited booths and tables.

On July 6, 1969, Casberg finished her shift and made her way into the seasonably cool evening air. She never made it to her parents' home, a small, lower level stick-built duplex at 3164 N. Bremen Street, in what is now known as the Riverwest neighborhood. Her father, Charlie Casberg, apparently wasn't overly concerned, as the family did not report her missing.

Things changed at about 1:30 p.m. on July 9, 1969, when a 10-year-old north side Milwaukee boy, fishing along the Root River on the Racine-Milwaukee County line with his father, Charles April, stumbled upon a large lump wrapped in the June 24 edition of the Milwaukee Sentinel. When April and his son unraveled the wet newspaper, they discovered the severed leg of what appeared to be a white female.

Charles April then went to an area near Eight Mile Road, where he contacted Robert Koenig, a grader operator for the town of Raymond. Koenig then contacted the Racine County Sheriff's Department.

Before long, law enforcement officers swarmed the area. It didn't take long to find other dismembered body parts. A head was found in a paper bag and, located a few feet away; two arms were each wrapped in editions of the Milwaukee Sentinel. Deputies discovered the limbs about 20 feet downhill from Eight Mile Road, just east of I-94, about seven feet south off a steel trestle condemned and closed to traffic since June 20.

Joseph Blessinger, the Racine County Sheriff at the time of grisly discovery, told the Milwaukee Sentinel that it looked as if "a butcher had done it.

"This is the most gruesome thing I've seen in my 30 years as sheriff," he said.

Racine County law enforcement conveyed the body parts to St. Mary's Hospital in Racine, where they were examined by a local pathologist. Dr. Myron Schuster determined that the woman died about two days earlier—on or about July 7. Schuster described the victim as a white woman, 20 or 21 years-of-age, with reddish-brown hair and freckles.

"The head, severed at the neck," the Milwaukee Sentinel notes, "had one pendulum, triangular bronze earring with a blue stone in the pierced left ear."

Authorities in Racine scoured missing persons' reports; however, only one—a woman missing from Milwaukee since located—matched the description of the murder victim.

Having heard news reports and the description of the head, Charlie Casberg contacted Milwaukee police. He told investigators that his daughter was last seen on Sunday, July 6 and that she might be the woman found on the banks of the Root River. Physical evidence soon confirmed the elder Casberg's worst fears.

As an intensive search of the river bank continued, police soon recovered a ripped-up photocopied picture of Stephanie Casberg lying alongside the road in the 8200 block of S. 68th Street in the city of Franklin, approximately seven-and-a-half miles northwest of the crime scene. To this day, even though Franklin as experienced substantial growth, this area is still relatively isolated— the Tuckaway Country Club to the west and a small subdivision to the east. Franklin detectives also located Stephanie's purse and a pink blanket in an "open area, not heavily wooded," although the specific location was not disclosed.

A check of maps of that era suggest that the suspect might have traveled Eight Mile Road to S. 27th Street; turned west on Ryan Road to S. 68th Street and then drove north to the 8200 block, where the photocopy was found.

Even though almost two dozen officers scoured the river bank, the young victim's torso and missing leg were not located.

But the case soon took a strange twist. On July 16, the body of a 34-year-old Pewaukee man was discovered just four blocks to the east of the Casberg crime scene. The man was found inside a red, 1962 Pontiac convertible. An apparent suicide, a hose was run from the car's exhaust into the vehicle.

Racine County detectives believe the man's suicide is not related to Casberg's murder. At the time, at least, Milwaukee detectives weren't so sure.

"Naturally," a high-ranking Milwaukee police source told the Milwaukee Sentinel, "when there's a man found dead so close to where her [Casberg's] remains were found and it looks like he may have committed suicide, the first question is why did he commit suicide and was there a connection?"

Based on the fact that Milwaukee police officials consider the case still cold, the 34-year-old Pewaukee man is probably no longer a suspect.

Racine County officials seem certain that the killer knew the area, although the Pewaukee man who committed suicide had no problems navigating the back roads of this relatively secluded location.

Nonetheless, as the years have passed, the murder of Stephanie Casberg turned stone cold.

SF's inquiry leads me to believe that the individual responsible for Stephanie Casberg's death is a white male, probably in his mid-to-late twenties at the time, in good physical shape in July 1969, with prior military experience. He may have served a tour in Vietnam. If he is still alive, the suspect is probably between 65 to 70 years-of-age. As a teenager, he probably resided in southern Milwaukee County.

SF is hopeful that someone out there—a relative, former spouse, or acquaintance of the suspect at the time—may now be willing to come forward so that one young woman's cry from the grave may finally get the hearing it deserves.

FREEDOM DIDN'T COME CHEAP FOR FORMER SAUKVILLE COPPER

FEBRUARY 5, 2011 AT 8:34 PM | FILED UNDER TRUE CRIME

Ask any detective worth is or her 'small badge' – as we call it in Milwaukee—and they will grudgingly admit that the individual freedoms many Americans enjoy are only as good as the abilities of the best defense attorneys.

Why?

Well, many police departments consistently revise their investigative procedures based on the challenges raised by the defense.

Milwaukee is home to several outstanding law firms and defense attorneys. Most will try to defuse criminal cases by attacking the evidence through legal proceedings initially filed at the Circuit Court level. These motions routinely contest the chain-of-custody of evidence, as well as the Constitutionality of items seized and the admissibility of statements made by defendants.

On rare occasions, when evidence is not suppressed and a plea deal will not suffice, cases make their way to a jury trial. Having testified and also chaired trials while at the assistant district attorney's table, a case that goes to a jury is considered—both by the state and the defense—a roll of the dice, although the stakes are typically higher for a defendant. After all, if the state loses a case at trial it really costs the taxpayers very little, even though the capabilities of the assistant DA may come into question. On the other hand, if the defense loses, their client is on the hook for a large legal bill and faces the likelihood of an even stiffer sentence. In the world of the trial court judges, if a defendant takes some of their time with a trial the judge is likely to take some of the defendant's time, on the back end, with a longer period of incarceration.

And courtroom observers will attest that those episodes of Perry Mason, where the defense usually prevails, are highly unrealistic, as prosecutors in Wisconsin typically triumph 90 percent of the time. Nonetheless, when a case does go to the jury room a defendant's freedom literally hangs in the balance.

Such was the case recently in Ozaukee County, Wisconsin, a well-heeled jurisdiction just to the north of Milwaukee, where a former police officer in the Village of Saukville contested charges of arson and second-degree recklessly endangering safety, which the state alleged occurred during her tour of duty.

"The verdict, which was announced at 8:25 p.m. Friday after more than four days of testimony," wrote Ozaukee Press reporter Bill Schanen IV, " ended a case that spanned more than two years and was replete with made-for-TV accusations — an dirty cop, a crime caught on tape and an interrogation that ended with a foot chase through the police station."

The case against former police officer, Melissa Kronebusch, 28, stemmed from a March 28, 2008, fire that occurred on a property adjacent to Saukville police headquarters. The state believed that Kronebush set fire to the house, set for demolition, so her boyfriend—a local firefighter—could get some reps extinguishing the blaze. Prosecutors alleged that grainy video footage depicted Kronebusch examining the structure just prior to the fire's discovery and then leave through a smoke filled parking lot.

Then, on June 26, 2008, when two investigators from the Wisconsin Department of Justice conducted an unannounced interview with Kornebusch, the officer supposedly fled on foot after agents accused her of starting the fire. Kronebusch, who was not under arrest at the time, was free to leave and/or invoke her right to an attorney, although the manner in which the interview was terminated seems rather bizarre.

But when confronted with a lengthy prison sentence, Kronebusch did one thing right: she retained Mike Guerin, a former Milwaukee police officer and, now, one of Wisconsin's elite defense attorneys, who did what outstanding defense attorneys do best at trial—he muddied the waters with reasonable doubt.

While investigators testified Kronebusch made contradictory statements, they failed to record the interview. Meanwhile, the defense team claimed their client's statements were consistent and that agents misrepresented a small snippet of the overall conversation. Moreover, the grainy video footage failed to provide a solid image of the officer.

To contest the allegation that Kronebusch drove through a smoke filled parking lot away from the fire, the defense put an expert witness on the stand.

"Defense witness John DeHaan, a forensic fire expert from Vallejo, Calif.," notes the Ozaukee Press, "testified that based on weather conditions at the time of the fire, the smoke would not have been blowing across the parking lot. He also cast doubt on whether the light seen at the back door of the house was from a flashlight [believed to be the officer's]."

The jury deliberated for almost seven hours before finding Kronebusch not guilty.

Of course, there are some in the community, especially the police haters, who reacted with outrage. As I noted in an earlier Spingola Files' post, however, circumstantial evidence is often ineffective, and can be spun in a way to make the innocent appear guilty.

When someone's liberty is one the line, prudence dictates that jurors, as well as members of the public, take a skeptical view of circumstantial evidence. During the prosecution of Kroenbusch, it appears that the Ozaukee County DA's office failed to rebut Mike Guerin's ability to shoot their theory full of just enough holes to sink the case. That is what elite defense attorney's do and you can bet that the price Melissa Kronebusch paid for her freedom did not come cheap.

THE DELAWARE DUMPSTER DEBACLE

FEBRUARY 1, 2011 AT 2:12 AM | FILED UNDER HOMICIDE

When conducting criminal investigations, detectives generally need to ascertain who committed the crime, what specifically occurred, where the incident took place, why the offense transpired and how the act evolved.

Two of these primary component questions—the 'who dun it' and 'why'—are often the most difficult to answer. At the end of the day, however, answering the question 'why' a crime-transpired may prove irrelevant when it comes to establishing the elements of an offense. For example, one can reasonably assume that a suspect robbed a bank because they wanted money. Why the person needed the cash is interesting to know but not necessary to find the perpetrator guilty.

During the ongoing investigation into the death of former presidential advisor John P. Wheeler, it is the 'why' question that has stirred the ever-simmering conspiracy pot.

On New Year's Eve, Wheeler's body fell from a garbage truck at a Delaware landfill. Investigators traced the trash to a ten-stop pick-up in nearby Newark, Delaware. Police canvassed the area and soon located a handful of people who had contact with Wheeler in the hours before his demise.

On December 29, an image of Wheeler, sporting a dark suit absent a necktie or jacket, appeared on surveillance video of a Wilmington, Delaware parking garage. He appeared confused while carrying a shoe in his left hand.

"I thought 'something is wrong here,'" the garage attendant, Kathleen Boyer, told New York Daily News reporter Helen Kennedy. Boyer explained that Wheeler appeared "disheveled" and claimed he was a victim of a robbery. Wheeler further told Boyer that he was looking for a Hertz rental car, even though his personal vehicle was later located just blocks away.

"He looked tired," Boyer told WTXF-TV in Philadelphia. "His eyes were very red. We didn't smell no alcohol," further explaining that she believed Wheeler had dementia.

Video evidence suggests that Wheeler's bizarre behavior carried on for at least another day. On December 30, investigators observed him on video inside a Wilmington building. The historic Nemours office complex is home to corporate giant DuPont, which has fueled conspiracy rumors.

A former Pentagon official, Wheeler worked for the federal government for decades and labored for three U.S. Presidents. Insiders considered him an expert on biological and chemical weapons. Nationally, Wheeler's efforts concerning the establishment of the Vietnam Veterans Memorial in Washington, D.C. are well known.

While detectives sorted through the details, police kept the circumstances involving Wheeler's death hush-hush. Yet in another strange turn of events, on January 28, the Delaware medical examiner's office released the cause of death, which apparently caught Newark police by surprise.

Without providing specifics, the ME's report notes that Wheeler died of blunt force trauma, which suggests he was struck in the head with a hard object and died from non-penetrating injuries. In plain English, Wheeler was likely bludgeoned to death. However, authorities have refused to release toxicology reports.

Did Wheeler sustain a head injury during a robbery? Was he under the influence of alcohol or drugs? Did he fall victim to an elaborate conspiracy?

Investigators are being tight-lipped, although I believe it is likely Mr. Wheeler may have stumbled into a situation where a couple of unsavory individuals realized a man, clearly out of his element, did not—for whatever reason—have his wits about him.

My hunch is that it was then that he was robbed-and-beaten. The perpetrators—and I believe there is more than one—dumped the body inside of a dumpster. The deposal points to a crime-of-opportunity robbery. After all, had an elaborate conspiracy taken place, similar to the disappearance of Jimmy Hoffa, why not dispose of the body permanently?

In the interim, this high profile investigation is bound to haunt Newark, Delaware police until those involved are apprehended. The Wheeler family is now offering a $25,000 cash reward for "information leading to the arrest of the killer." Twenty-five Gs is a lot of money for those living a hard life on the streets. My guess is it will not take long for someone to drop the proverbial dime.

COLLATERAL DAMAGE: HOMICIDE SUSPECT'S SON GETS A PINK SLIP

MARCH 5, 2011 AT 5:30 PM | FILED UNDER COP TALK

Police officers come from diverse backgrounds and hold various political views. Put ten law enforcement managers in a room to discuss a particular issue facing an agency and a fly on the wall may hear six or seven different responses.

Yet, when discussing the homicide case involving retired Bolingbrook, Illinois Police Sergeant Drew Peterson, the overwhelming consensus of current and former police officers is that the man is guilty as sin.

Drew Peterson is currently sitting in jail awaiting trial for the homicide of his third wife, Kathleen Savio. The couple married in 1992, just two months after Peterson divorced his second wife, Victoria. The relationship soured in October of 2003, when Peterson began dating Stacy Coles. A bitter battle ensued over the couple's two sons and the division of assets.

Just eight days after his divorce from Savio, Drew Peterson, 49, married Stacy Coles, who was just 19-years-old at the time.

Things got even uglier on March 1, 2004, when Drew Peterson arrived at Savio's home to dropped-off the couple's sons. Peterson found the door locked and received no response when he knocked. A trained police officer, Peterson did not force entry or call the local police for assistance. Instead, he contacted a locksmith. With the door open, Peterson allowed a neighbor woman to enter the home first; whereupon, the woman discovered Savio's bloody body in a dry bathtub. The Illinois State Police then conducted an investigation, based, in part, on the conclusions of the Will County Coroner's jury—a group of lay people, who, based on the coroners' presentation, concluded that Savio's death was an accident.

Even though the EMT's at the scene suspected foul play in Savio's death, things soon returned to normal for Peterson — until October 29, 2007, when Peterson's fourth wife, Stacy, came-up missing. Law enforcement officials believe that Stacy Peterson is likely dead, although her body has yet to be located.

With wife number four in the wind and Fox News' Greta Van Susteren giving Stacy's disappearance national attention, the Illinois State Police reopened the Savio case. After authorities exhumed Savio's body, it took two independent forensic pathologists less than an hour to classify her death as a homicide.

But a break in the case did not stem from the work of Illinois investigators. Instead, it was information developed by former LAPD Detective Mark Fuhrman—on consignment for Fox News—that broke the Savio investigation wide-open.

Realizing that investigators from the Illinois State Police had failed to do some simple legwork, Fuhrman interviewed Peterson's ex-wives. Drew Peterson's second wife, Victoria, told Fuhrman her ex-husband attended locksmith school and typically carried his tools with him. This would explain the lack of a forced entry at Savio's residence. Moreover, as a police officer and a locksmith, Peterson was likely aware that forensic investigators might seize and then examine Savio's door locks. Once a certified locksmith opened the door, however, these actions forever altered the crime scene.

Smelling a rat, Fuhrman dug even deeper. He then located and interviewed Stacy Peterson's minister. Hoping that Stacy was still alive, the minister, due to confidentiality concerns, had refused to come forward. Fuhrman convinced the minister that investigators needed access to any information provided by the missing woman. The minister eventually told Fuhrman that, the night prior to the discovery of Savio's body, Stacy confided that she awoke and discovered that Drew Peterson was not home. Stacy called Drew's cell phone but received no answer. She then went to the first level of the couple's Bolingbrook home, where she found Drew Peterson—dressed in all black—stuffing another woman's clothes into the washer.

According to minister, Drew looked at Stacy and said, 'You know where I've been. I was taking care of the problem. It'll be a perfect crime.'

Unfortunately, with Stacy Peterson missing, the statements made to the minister are hearsay, which is typically not admissible in court. In response, the Illinois legislature passed a bill, some call Drew's Law, which enables these types of hearsay statements as evidence. Many legal scholars believe the law is probably unconstitutional and will not withstand a legal challenge.

Now, you may ask, why is SF rehashing the details of the Drew Peterson case?

Like many high profile crimes, the investigation into the death of Kathleen Savio and the disappearance of Stay Peterson sometimes results in collateral damage to those on the periphery. In this instance, one individual caught in the middle of a huge and embarrassing investigation is Drew Peterson's 31-year-old son, Stephen.

Last month, the Oak Brook Police and Fire Commission, on a vote of 3-0, terminated the employment of Police Officer Stephen Peterson, for allegedly obstructing the investigation into the disappearance of his father's fourth wife, Stacy.

Even though many veteran officers have little doubt about Drew Peterson's guilt, some are of the opinion that Stephen Peterson was targeted not because of what he did but because Drew Peterson is his father.

According to news sources, in the days preceding the disappearance of Stacy, Drew Peterson provided his son, Stephen, with three firearms and $236,800. On its face, neither of these transfers is unlawful. In fact, authorities have not charged Stephen Peterson with any crime. However, the chairman of the Oak Brook Police and Fire Commission, Frederick Cappetta, views Stephen Peterson's actions as "self-serving, disingenuous, not credible." Stephen Peterson, on the other hand, is of the opinion that commission, or any other law enforcement body, has yet to prove that the firearms and/or the money were relevant to any criminal investigation.

As of this writing, Stephen Peterson's claim appears legitimate, although one will never know the relevance of the firearms until Stacy Peterson's body is located and examined.

That being said many law enforcement veterans are skeptical of decisions rendered by civilian oversight boards, whose make-up consists of handpicked, mayoral appointees. The cynical view is that commission members are generally political soul mates of the mayor and/or are susceptible to political pressure. As such, some believe police and fire commissions simply act as rubber stamps delivering the desired outcome for the political establishment. The old adage that whoever controls the machinery controls the outcome is, in many instances, reality, even though many of the ivory tower-types claim otherwise.

"When I gave Steve my guns there was no investigation to impede," Peterson said in a statement through his attorney. "They were my favorite guns, and I was going to give them to Steve when I retired anyway. I only gave him three of the dozen or so guns I owned, and I kept most of my guns in my house and the police confiscated them all, so how could giving him those three guns impede anything?"

Stephen Peterson's attorney expressed outrage at the Oak Brook Police and Fire Commission's decision. "We're disappointed, but not surprised," attorney Tamara Cummings told the Chicago Tribune. "This board is a kangaroo court, for lack of a better word."

Is Stephen Peterson a victim of a political game of guilt by association or was he rightfully terminated?

Only time and the discovery of Stacy Peterson's body will tell.

In the interim, Stephen Peterson is appealing his termination to DuPage County Circuit Court.

THE FOG OF TIME & GRAFTON CRIMES
APRIL 23, 2011 AT 9:33 PM | FILED UNDER HOMICIDE

Having spent a fair amount of time doing research on older homicides, I find that local libraries, not the Internet, are often the best resources for information. Even though the lingering body odor of homeless men using the second floor restroom of the Milwaukee Public Library as a changing station might singe the nostrils of unknowing visitors, sifting through newspaper articles on microfilm better enables a reader to grasp the totality of a specific period of time as events unfold.

While reading newspaper articles from 30, 40 or 50-years ago, I am frequently amazed at the depth of reporting, as well as the fact that some very horrific crimes—like the reporters and detectives of that era—soon fade away into oblivion.

On occasion, I stumble onto an interesting case and wonder, knowing that a generation of investigators have retired and likely passed away; did anyone bother to connect the dots between crimes that occurred many years apart?

About a year-and-a-half ago, I profiled the tragic death of a young boy on my former blog, From the Notebook of a Homicide Detective.

Without rehashing all the facts, investigators believe a probable stranger abducted Brad Machett from a blue-collar Milwaukee neighborhood. On October 31, 1980, while taking a shortcut to school, two boys came upon the ten-year-old victim in a Town of Grafton field. Detectives determined that the killer sodomized and later strangled Machett, whose homicide remains unsolved.

On October 24, 2009, Fox News 6 in Milwaukee reported that detectives were taking a fresh look at the Machett case. Unfortunately, potential biological evidence succumbed to both father time and the packing techniques at a time when DNA analysis was little more than a science fiction fantasy.

Yet one has to believe that the monster who murdered Brad Machett did not simply fall back into line. Sexual killers typically develop fantasies that sometimes take years to act on. Once they kill, these types of perpetrators go through a cooling-off period; however, somewhere down the line, they need to fulfill their raging fantasies by pursuing additional victims.

Over the course of the past three-decades, investigators developed theories as to the identity and whereabouts of the Machett suspect: the killer was a transient; he might have gone to prison for another crime; became a victim of foul play himself; committed suicide or simply died of natural causes.

Late last week, during another visit to the library, I stumbled upon a case that shares some eerie similarities to the Machett homicide, although this murder occurred during the latter part of the Eisenhower administration.

On April 4, 1959, at about 6:15 p.m., six-year-old Ben Wagner, in the company of his neighborhood friend, Christ Wilhelm, cut through an alley of their north side Milwaukee neighborhood, near N. 22nd and W. Chambers Streets, en route to buy ice cream from a nearby store. A blue and white Plymouth station wagon suddenly approached the boys and asked if they needed a ride. When Ben Wagner said they did not, a man grabbed the young boy and pulled him inside.

Only six-years-old, Christ Wilhelm apparently did not put two-and-two together. Almost two hours later, when Ben failed to return home with ice cream, his family formed a search party. Knocking at a door across the alley at 2967-A N. 21st Street—the address of the Wilhelm family—Ben's parents, Louis and Shirley Wagner, realized their worst nightmare: their son had entered a stranger's vehicle.

At about the same time Christ Wilhelm provided the Wagners with the chilling details, Milton Geiger, 38, drove his wife, Mary Lu, and his son, Douglas, south on Highway 141, as the family journeyed home from a tour of flood-ravaged Saukville, a small town 25 miles north of their Milwaukee home. As Geiger drove past a blue and white Plymouth station wagon, he observed a young boy frantically waiving from inside. Believing something was awry, Geiger turned and began pursuing the station wagon, but lost sight of the Plymouth near Brown Deer Road, about two-and-a-half miles north of the border of Milwaukee County.

Geiger then returned home. He later contacted police after hearing news reports of a young boy's abduction. With Milwaukee Police Department Detective Sgt. Orville Youss in tow, Geiger returned to the scene near Brown Deer Road, but, as investigators arrived, they received word that authorities in Ozaukee County located a boy's body in the Town of Grafton.

On April 5, at 6:17 a.m., newspaper delivery driver Donald Frazen, 28, believed he spotted a rag doll lying in a watery ditch on Lake Shore Road just five feet from the pavement and 348 feet north of the entrance to the estate of Erwin C. Uihlein, the President of the Joseph Schlitz Brewing Company. Franzen exited his car and found the body of Ben Wagner fully clothed and covered in blood. Even in death, the young boy clinched his ice cream money—a nickel and two pennies—in his left hand. Frazen observed another 31 cents on the nearby ground.

Ozaukee County Sheriff Roland Schafer conveyed Ben Wagner's body to Port Washington, where Milwaukee County Medical Examiner L.J. Van Hecke immediately performed an autopsy. "Throttle marks" where located around the young boy's neck suggesting strangulation was attempted. The killer stabbed his victim three times under the left armpit, but the cause of death was a deep wound to the center of the chest that severed a major artery.

Although Ben Wagner's body showed no signs of molestation, Milwaukee Police Lieutenant Leo Woerful theorized that suspect might have killed in haste after the brief car chase with Milton Geiger. While at the Town of Grafton crime scene, Geiger told authorities he believed the boy lying in the ditch was the same person he spotted frantically waiving from inside the blue and white Plymouth station wagon.

The following day detectives suggested a link between the Wagner homicide and a sexual assault at south side Milwaukee tavern. Earlier in the day on April 4, 1959, a white male, described as 25-years-of-age with bushy hair committed an "unnatural sex act" with a boy in a tavern washroom.

Thirteen years prior to the development of the FBI's Behavior Science Unit, a reporter at the Milwaukee Journal sought to develop a profile of Ben Wagner's assailant. Dr. Michael Kasak, a local psychiatrist, told the newspaper that the young boy's killer is a "deviate, sexual or otherwise" and suffers from "algolagnia," described as "a lust for pain." Dr. Kasak believed the perpetrator a "sadist"—a word emanating from France's Marquis de Sade, who allegedly tortured "youngsters" and others at his castle and took joy in observing the suffering of others.

After an extensive search of public records at the Milwaukee Public Library, SF was unable to ascertain if Ben Wagner's homicide was resolved with an official clearance. A handful of informal inquires will hopefully result in an answer in the near future.

THE KILLER CONUNDRUM

MAY 21, 2011 AT 4:15 PM | FILED UNDER HOMICIDE

Some might argue that times were much simpler 47-years-ago. Families typically sat down, together, for evening meals and actually spoke to one another. Absent Facebook and cellular telephones, teenagers had a difficult time covertly communicating over the party telephone lines, where neighbors could easily ease drop on conversations.

Unfortunately, for the families of murder victims, the days of yore bring back chilling memories of lenient justice.

In 1964, with Earl Warren as its chief justice, the U.S. Supreme Court built upon the foundation it had laid pertaining to the rights of the accused (i.e. criminal defendants).

The Warren court championed the exclusionary rule (Mapp v. Ohio, 1961); held that the Sixth Amendment afforded publicly funded legal counsel to indigent persons charged with any serious crime (Gideon v. Wainwright, 1963); and required law enforcement officers to read any person being interrogated their Fifth and Sixth Amendment rights (Miranda v. Arizona, 1966).

Moreover, the Warren court, as well as state legislatures throughout the nation, ushered in an era of juvenile justice reform — responsible for the commonly used phrase, 'treated with kid gloves.'

In the 1960s, juveniles found adjudicated of violent homicides—the courts frown upon using the term 'convicted' in cases involving children—were often released upon reaching 21-years-of-age.

Jim Stingl, a columnist for the Milwaukee Journal Sentinel, spotlighted such a case in his April 30, 2011, column.

In the summer of 1964, Janette Kruzyski, an 11-year-old south side Milwaukee girl, took a bike ride to Kosciuszko Park, where children—prior to the proliferation of air conditioning—beat the summer heat by using the county swimming pool. She eventually ran into a 15-year-old boy, who offered to take her for a ride on tandem bicycle. Things got ugly when the boy attempted for sexually force himself upon Janette. When the girl resisted, the boy used rocks to crush Janette's skull.

Since children's court proceedings typically exclude members of the public, the actual name of the 15-year-old boy, identified in documents as "J.S.," remain under seal. Records indicate that J.S. received a term on incarceration at Ethan Allen School for Boys—ironically, just blocks away from Spingola Files HQ, which means the system probably released "J.S." around 1970.

"A judge ruled that the young killer was sane," wrote Stingl. "A psychiatrist testified that the boy faced so-called irresistible impulses."

While criminologists offer differing arguments concerning the terms of incarceration for violent juvenile offenders, most would agree that the perpetrators of sexual homicides typically experience bizarre fantasies that intensify to a point of action. After acting upon these fantasies, killers generally go through a so-called cooling-off period, until the urges return and they reoffend.

Which leaves one to wonder: whatever happened to J.S.? Since the court documents identifying the killer remain under sealed, was local law enforcement ever notified that a sexual murderer—currently about 62-years-of-age—relocated to their community?

Over the years, the Warren court's members aged and were replaced by the crime control oriented justices of the Burger Court; then the increasingly conservative members of the Rehnquist court. Many legal scholars believe the U.S. Supreme Court's current chief justice, John Roberts, is even more conservative than Rehnquist, the late Shorewood native.

The charging of the guard throughout our nation's courts has also brought about a much different philosophical outlook related to juvenile justice.

Just yesterday, the Wisconsin Supreme Court issued a landmark ruling regarding the sentencing of juveniles in homicide cases.

Almost eleven-years-ago, a jury convicted Omar Ninham of killing 13-year-old Zong Vang. The details of the crime paint a picture of a sadistic individual.

"The record revealed that Ninham, 14 years old at the time," notes Wisconsin State Bar Legal Writer Joe Forward, "dropped Vang to his ultimate death from a multi-story parking garage in Green Bay after tormenting him with friends and dangling him over the wall's edge by Vang's ankles.

"Before trial, Ninham threatened the life of a witness and a circuit court judge, and threatened to rape another witness. A presentence investigation found that Ninham was a serious substance abuser, drank alcohol every day, and lived in an extremely dysfunctional family structure."

Fearful that a violent sociopath that might reoffend, the Circuit Court judge sentenced Ninham to life without the possibility of parole.

Just last year, In Graham v. Florida, the U.S. Supreme Court prohibited sentences of juvenile offenders—specifically those tried as adults—to life without the possibility of parole for non-homicidal offenses.

In a five-to-two ruling, the Wisconsin Supreme Court noted the homicide exception in Graham, and, therefore, concluded that Ninham should remain incarcerated for life.

Ninham's attorneys vow to appeal the ruling to the U.S. Supreme Court, arguing that requiring a 14-year-old offender to serve a life sentence violates the Eighth Amendment's prohibition against "cruel and unusual punishment."

Yet one if left to ponder the cruel and unusual punishments melted out to Janette Kruzyski and Zong Zang, as neither—unlike their killers—had the ability to contest their death sentences.

LEAVING FOR COLLEGE?
TAKE SOME COMMON SENSE ALONG, TOO

AUGUST 27, 2011 AT 5:02 PM | FILED UNDER CITIZEN TALK

Around this time of year—in what has become an educational rite of passage—millions of young Americans arrive for the first time or return to college campuses around the nation.

After unloading the trailer or truck at the curb adjacent to a dorm or an apartment building, the parents of these students smile and wave goodbye, hoping and praying that the ones they love avoid becoming a statistic.

Before simply waving goodbye and hoping for the best, if your son or daughter will not heed the advice of their parents (a character trait pervasive throughout America), refer them to this Spingola Files' posting.

Typically, when college students meet their demise alcohol is in the mix. Here in Wisconsin, the homicide of a 22-year-old college student serves as a prime example. On June 23, 2007, Kelly Nolan walked away from Amy's Café in downtown Madison around 11:30 p.m. with an employee of a tavern—a man who later claimed to have passed the young woman off to another individual.

Two weeks later, Nolan's decomposing body was located in the town of Dunn, about 12 miles south of Madison. Using state-of-the-art technology from a federally funded intelligence Fusion Center, investigators pinged the young woman's cellular telephone to locate her remains. Sources say that Nolan's partying lifestyle has made it difficult to connect the dots. Her killer remains at large.

Moreover, alcohol, once again, figures into the equation of two recent disappearances of young, college-aged women.

Not far from the campus of Indiana University, twenty-year-old college student Lauren Spierer went missing on June 3. On the night she disappeared, Spierer was accompanied by three men, one of whom, media sources claim, is her boyfriend. Police believe alcohol played a role in her disappearance. Investigators continue to search a landfill for the 4-foot, eleven-inch woman's remains.

On the west coast, 23-year-old Darlene Carlson disappeared on August 6 after leaving Finnegan's Pub in Stockton, California. According to friends, she continued making phone calls until 5 a.m. Friends from the pub told investigators Carlson, or someone else using her cell phone, replied to a text message at 11 a.m. Once again, Carlson's lifestyle, police believe, is making it difficult to develop an adequate investigative timeline, although cellular telephone surveillance equipment, operated by the Northern California Regional Terrorism Threat Assessment Center, will certainly play a role in the overall investigation.

While foul play is the likely culprit in the cases involving these missing women, college males are no strangers to alcohol-fueled tragedies as well.

La Crosse, Wisconsin, is college town with a reputation for hard drinking. Since 1997, nine men have drowned in the Mississippi River. Some locals speculate that a serial killer lured drunken college-aged males to the banks of the river and shoved the inebriated men over the side. Three years ago, two former New York City detectives believed the "smiley face" serial killer was at work, while La Crosse police officials named three suspects: Jack Daniels, Jim Beam and Captain Morgan.

Then on February 14, 2010, 21-year-old Craig Meyers disappeared after a leaving a downtown La Crosse tavern at 1:50 a.m. According the La Crosse Tribune, police discovered Meyers' footprints leading from a snow bank "between the Marriott Courtyard and the Riverside Center Buildings out onto ice-crusted river." On February 15, a cadaver dog traced Meyers' scent through the six-inch ice. The next day, divers found Meyers' body 15 feet from shore in about 25 feet of water. Depending on which test results one chooses to believe, Meyers' blood alcohol content ranged from 0.19 to 0.28—two to three times over the legal limit to operate a motor vehicle in Wisconsin.

So parents and friends, during the next week or two, make sure someone that your college bound son or daughter will listen to gives them some timely advice.

In the interim, SF has some tips for those making the trek to a college town USA.

Late last winter, during a Law Enforcement Career Day event at the University of Wisconsin—Platteville, I profiled the case of a Milwaukee woman abducted from the city's eastside and, later, bludgeoned to death. Unfortunately, long hair—as beautiful as it may be—also serves as a means of control. I am not suggesting that women sport Sinéad O'Connor-type hairstyles; however, the less there is to grab the better.

Here is another tip that might be easier to abide by—while socializing, never leave a drink, alcoholic or otherwise, unattended. One veteran officer recently told me of a case involving a female college student who woke-up in her bed alone. She noticed her panties turned inside out and contacted the police. Investigators found six used prophylactics in a nearby garbage container. DNA testing determined that the semen left inside belonged to six different men. The last thing the young woman recalled was drinking at a tavern less than a mile away. Whether it was an over indulgence of alcohol or a substance placed in her drink, the subsequent blackout—even if suspects are developed—makes it virtually impossible to prove the sexual activity was not consensual.

Remember, it is important to think before you drink. When socializing, stay in a group. Then make sure that all members of the group remain together throughout the night and make it home in one piece. If someone disappears, make an all-out effort to locate the missing party. Should a member of a group decide to leave with another person, know the identity of the person(s) they are leaving with by obtaining names and verified cell phone numbers.

Follow these simple tips and, more importantly, if choosing to drink, do so moderately. After finding a decomposing body in a woods or a bloated corpse in a river, investigators routinely hear the following from the next of kin:

- If only she had stayed with her friends.

- Why didn't she tell the members of her group where she was going?

- Why did his so-called friends let him walk away that drunk?

- Why didn't anyone search for her after she disappeared from the group?

INVESTIGATORS WATCH AS SUPREME COURT TAKES-UP GPS CASE

OCTOBER 23, 2011 AT 2:45 PM | FILED UNDER THE COURTS

The new term of the U.S. Supreme Court is set to begin. On the docket is the case of the United States v. Jones. From all corners of the country, Investigators are keeping close tabs on this case to see if the nation's highest court will continue to rubber stamp America's surveillance society.

In the Jones case, investigators used a GPS tracking device attached to the car of the suspect, Antoine Jones, for over a month absent a court order. Based, in part, on the GPS data, Jones was later convicted of distributing a kilo of cocaine. While researching the case, it appears the device was attached to Jones' car while the vehicle was parked in a quasi-public place.

Since 1925, in the case of Carroll v. the United States, our nation's highest court has generally concluded that a motor vehicle's mobility and use of public roadways equates to a lesser expectation of privacy under the Fourth Amendment's reasonableness requirement.

But high-level jurists, fearful of an increasingly intrusive government, believe technology used by law enforcement, absent a court order, cries out for Fourth Amendment protections.

Early last spring, Judge Diane Wood, of the U.S. 7th Court of Appeals in Chicago, noted that the methods investigators currently use to retrieve Global Positioning System data would "make the system that George Orwell depicted in his famous novel, '1984,' seem clumsy."

In August, Brooklyn, New York, Federal Judge Nicholas G. Garaufis shot-down a request from investigators to retrieve 113 days of data from cellular telephone towers, describing such a search as "an Orwellian intrusion."

Clearly, the U.S. Supreme Court took the Jones case to examine how the government's use of modern technology relates to the Fourth Amendment.

As a former homicide detective, I do not find the use of GPS technology in the Jones case particularly troubling. If, however, investigators entered Jones' secured garage to attached the GPS device, I believe the entry, absent a court order, would constitute an unreasonable search.

More troubling is the government's tracking of average Americans via cellular telephone with the use of GPS monitoring or Stingray pinging technology. In these cases, government lawyers argue that GPS and pinging signals are byproducts of private cellular telephone infrastructures and, as such, are not personal effects; thereby, exempting these searches from Fourth Amendment scrutiny.

The Fourth Amendment, however, specifically notes that, "The right of the people to be secure in their persons, houses, papers, and effects, against unreasonable searches and seizures" shall not be violated.

Does anyone—absent an employee of a Big Brother government agency or an Orwellian jurist—honestly believe an individual's cellular telephone is not an effect; that this effect was purchased by an individual; and, without the signal offered by this effect, the government would be unable to obtain the desired data?

In an earlier post, SF noted that it is the investigation of an alleged computer hacker, currently being litigated at the federal district court level, not the Jones case that will provide the telling details of what, if any, civil liberties, Americans might retain.

In the interim, SF encourages its readers to call their legislators in the House of Representatives and the U.S. Senate and ask them to support a bill authored by Rep. Jason Chaffetz (R-Utah) and Sen. Ron Wyden (D-Oregon), which would prohibit government agents from using GPS or other cellular phone geo-location data to track Americans absent a court order.

SPEAKERS AVAILABLE TO DISCUSS MILWAUKEE-BASED CRIME NOVEL

Frequent visitors to SF are keenly aware that I have touted The Cozen Protocol, Mitchell Nevin's well researched, yet fictional book about a Milwaukee gang war and an ensuring police corruption scandal.

http://www.wuwm.com/programs/lake_effect/le_sgmt.php?segmentid=7966

Late Friday, I received a note from the novel's publisher indicating that former law enforcement veterans are now available to review and discuss the book at group events. The cost, I've been told, is predicated upon the travel expenses of the facilitator.

For more information, e-mail **livia@badgerwordsmith.com**

SHOOTING AT THE OK(AUCHEE) CORRAL STILL UNDER REVIEW

OCTOBER 8, 2011 AT 3:41 PM | FILED UNDER CITIZEN TALK

In early September, SF shined a spotlight on the shooting of a prowler by a homeowner in Qkauchee, Wisconsin. About three weeks later, the Waukesha County Sheriff's Department released the 9-1-1 tape of the call from the shooter, Mike Fitzsimmons.

Dispatch: "What's your problem there?"

Caller: "Someone was in my garage. They ran out, they wouldn't, they were attacking me, so I shot him."

Dispatch: "You shot him?" [with a .357 magnum with hollow point rounds]

Caller: "I think the f***** is dead."

Dispatch: "Where'd you hit him?"

Caller: "Twice in the chest."

Dispatch: "Twice in the chest?"

Caller: "Once I shot him, the back door was locked."

Dispatch: "Ok."

Caller: "So I came back around the front and grabbed the phone. Now I'm going back, I don't want to touch nothing."

Dispatch: "Is he moving at all?"

Caller: "Umm.."

Dispatch: "Or have you been by him at all?"

Caller: "He's on the back deck, I'm on the front."

The investigation is still not complete. The Wisconsin Regional Crime Lab is examining a key piece of evidence—a round that lodged in the deck as it passed through the body of James Babe.

Yet 9-1-1 recordings, made, unedited in real time, in the immediate aftermath of an incident, sometimes provide insight into the mindset of a victim or a suspect.

Are Fitzsimmons' own words to the 9-1-1 call center that, "Someone was in my garage. They ran out, they wouldn't, they were attacking me, so I shot him," indicative that he embellished his statement—as if to say 'they wouldn't stop'—mid-sentence? Or are these the excited utterances of a man under stress who feared for his life?

The Hells' Angels have a motto proclaiming, "Two men can keep a secret if two are dead." Neither SF nor Waukesha County investigators were present when the shooting occurred. The prowler, James Babe, is dead. Therefore, the physical evidence—the round and wood fragments recovered from the deck—is being scrutinized to the nth degree. One can bet that ballistic experts, physicists, and a possible botanist, will check the wood and measure the speed and projection of the round as it entered and passed through Babe's body.

While researching this incident, SF stumbled upon this posted comment:

"FACTS: James Babe broke into another mans home. He was not shot in the blackened garage or in the back (leaving). He was shot in the chest, fell backwards and was on the rear deck. Conclusion: Babe was coming after Mike. Mike is INNOCENT! Case closed!"

In reality, however, the aforementioned comment does not reflect the current state of the law in Wisconsin.

Legally, citizens and police officers may employ the use of deadly force in self-defense if they fear for their life or the life of another. The purpose of using deadly force is to stop the actions of the perpetrator.

If the first shot fired by Fitzsimmons knocked Babe the deck and Babe no was longer a threat, then the second shot might fall outside the scope of lawful use of deadly force in self-defense. If, however, Babe still posed a threat, as Fitzsimmons' alleges in his statement, the second shot might fall under the purview of the self-defense doctrine.

Hypothetically, if physical evidence illustrates that a suspect was lying on his or her back and a second round was then deploy, even though the suspect's ability to threaten the shooter had ceased, the second round might fall outside the self-defense doctrine.

As of November 1, 2011, law-abiding Wisconsin residents over 21-years-of-age can apply for permits to carry concealed weapons. The shooting at the QK(auchee) corral should serve as a prime example of the kind of scrutiny one should expect when deadly force is employed.

One person who recently finished a concealed carry training class related that an instructor told those in attendance that simply removing a concealed firearm in public might cost as much as $5,000 to $10,000 in legal fees once law enforcement initiates an investigation.

Just because the law will soon give law-abiding citizens the means to defend themselves, does not mean taking action with a firearm is the most prudent way to proceed. Sit back and think for a moment: wouldn't Mike Fitzsimmons' life—both mentally and financially—be far less complicated, right now, had he simply locked the doors to his residence and called the police?

Note: After reviewing this case in its entirety, the Waukesha County District Attorney's Office ruled the shooting of Babe as justifiable self-defense.

PREDATOR SPY DRONES: HOVERING ABOVE YOUR TOWN SOON?

DECEMBER 11, 2011 AT 12:59 PM | FILED UNDER CITIZEN TALK

In his book, It is Dangerous to be Right When the Government is Wrong, former Judge Andrew Napolitano notes that citizens in a free society possess certain inalienable, God given rights. The use of intrusive technology to conduct government surveillance of the populace for surveillance sake, absent a court order, Napolitano suggests, is the antithesis of the ideals of the founding fathers.

Since 2005, the political class in the United States has tossed the Bill of Rights to the wind by rubber stamping a $500 billion domestic surveillance infrastructure. Termed 'intelligence fusion centers,' seventy-two high tech monitoring centers, funded by the Department of Homeland Security and operated with inadequate, trust-based oversight—routinely harvests the personal financial data of hundreds-of-thousands of Americans, uses sophisticated technology to monitor the cellular telephones of millions of Americans, and photographs and records the movements of everyday people involved in non-criminal activities.

Most Americans seem ambivalent to the reality that their own tax dollars, as well as billions of dollars borrowed from overseas to underwrite the U.S. federal deficit, are being used to monitor their e-mails, text messages, financial transactions, and, in real time— if so desired—their cellular telephone movements.

But it gets even worse.

Yesterday, the Los Angeles Times reported that Predator Droves— unmanned spy planes used to locate and destroy enemy combatants in Afghanistan, Pakistan, and recently to spy on Iran—are now being used to monitor American citizens absent a court order.

Another report at RT.com strongly suggests that the deployment of drones to conduct domestic spy operations within the United States is inevitable.

http://rt.com/usa/news/us-drones-border-patrol-489/

Prior to 9-11, the military's involvement in domestic law enforcement was, for good reason, limited by law. Predator Drones operated by the armed forces of the United States have several unique capabilities, one of which is the use of inferred technology, which can read individual license plates from 12,000 feet and monitor the activities inside of private residences protected by the Fourth Amendment. Sophisticated telephoto optics enable Predator Drones to act as airborne window peepers, even though an area around private residences might be considered curtilage—a barrier area of sorts where courts generally extend a reasonable expectation of privacy.

For those who believe that the scans and pat downs conducted by the TSA are overly intrusive, with drones hovering above, 'You 'ain't seen nothin' yet.'

Of course, when confronted with the use of Big Brother technology, government officials will once again ask the public to place trust in a handful of faceless bureaucrats to provide oversight, which, in the past, has resulted in supporters of U.S. Presidential candidate Ron Paul and others engaged in First Amendment political activities being placed on a government watch lists.

Even though our nation is running a $1.35 trillion dollar annual federal government deficit, our political leaders, like J. Edgar Hoover before them, appear so intent of gathering and maintaining data on ordinary Americans that they are willing to spend the nation into oblivion. In the interim, we are left to ask, what ever happened to the Bill of Rights and the concept of limited government?

CONSTITUTION 1, BIG BROTHER 0—TOP OF THE SECOND

JANUARY 24, 2012 AT 3:37 AM | FILED UNDER THE COURTS

Earlier today, in a rare unanimous ruling, the U.S. Supreme Court prohibited law enforcement from installing GPS tracking equipment to monitor the movements of Americans absent an order from a judge.

The ruling is a shot across the bow of the ever-expanding government surveillance state.

"The Obama administration argued that getting one [a court order] could be cumbersome, perhaps impossible in the early stages of an investigation," said a report from the Associated Press.

But probable cause—the legal requirement needed to obtain a court order—is not a difficult threshold to meet. Otherwise, all the police would need to spy on American citizens is an unsubstantiated hunch.

Reading between the lines it appears that the justices of the U.S. Supreme Court are skeptical of the government's use of intrusive technologies. Police agencies are already experimenting with equipment that searches individuals—absent a reasonable suspicion—as they simply walk down the street.

http://techland.time.com/2012/01/20/police-developing-tech-to-virtually-frisk-people-from-82-feet-away/

ONLY time will tell how the courts come down on the monitoring of Americans' movements via cellular telephone tracking technology.

SF REVIEWS "AMERICAN STASI: FUSION CENTERS AND DOMESTIC SPYING."

JANUARY 21, 2012 AT 8:09 PM | FILED UNDER BOOK REVIEW

A MAGAZINE EXPOSÉ REIVEW

Title: American Stasi: Fusion Centers and Domestic Spying

Author: Miles Kinard

Genre: Non-fiction—Government, Crime & Ethics

As a former homicide detective, I am very skeptical of conspiracy theories. The sheer number of people working in concert to pull-off such elaborate schemes leads me to believe that those complicit in the planning and/or execution of such events would confide with someone who, prior to or after the fact, would notify authorities.

In my new book, Best of the Spingola Files, I profiled the 2010 drowning death of 21-year-old Craig Meyers. Police reported that Meyers' blood alcohol content was over three times the legal limit to drive when he fell through the ice on the Mississippi River. However, since nine other young men have met similar fates in the hard-drinking college town of La Crosse, Wisconsin, over the last 15 years, plenty of people still believe that a serial killer is lying in wait to push only male drunks into the fast moving river. The problem is that—when asked—these conspiracy theorists cannot provide the name of a single witness or possible suspect, nor find any surveillance footage of the alleged perpetrator.

Yet some theories considered outside the mainstream actually have some creditability. In these instances, though, the alleged conspiracy is not really a conspiracy—the names, the faces, and the events are right there, in plain sight, for the willing to see. Miles Kinard's magazine exposé, American Stasi: Fusion Centers and Domestic Spying, is a prime example.

For over ten years now, some wing-nut organizations have alleged that the U.S. government orchestrated the attacks of 9/11 in order to seize the civil liberties of Americans. Some even suggest that Vice President Cheney had a hand in the conspiracy so as to boost the profits of Halliburton. Yet, as is the case in La Crosse, these theorists cannot provide a single document or a creditable witness to make their square peg fit into a round hole.

Instead, in the aftermath of the 9/11 attacks, President Bush, and others with only good intentions in mind, sought to ensure that another such attack would never again occur on American soil. Unfortunately, when government money flows too freely, things often go awry.

In his 1996 book, On Social Structure and Science, sociologist Robert Merton lists the five possible causes for unintended consequences:

- Ignorance;

- An error in analysis;

- Immediate interests that override long-term interests;

- Basic values, such as rigid ideological views or other beliefs, that results in unfavorable, long-term consequences;

- Self-defeating prophecies that result in an ant being killed with a sledgehammer.

One such example of the theory of unintended consequences is Aid to Families with Dependent Children (AFDC), which began in 1935 to assist those in need through the depths of the Great Depression. The elected officials who initially supported this program probably never realized that AFDC would undermine the nation's work ethic by creating a culture of entitlement.

The American surveillance state is another example of good intentions gone badly. Just 45-days after the 9/11 attacks, the USA Patriot Act sailed to passage. With congressional approval, the Bush administration gave the bureaucracy a virtual blank check to create a domestic spy apparatus so intrusive that U.S. Appellate Judge Daine Wood noted it "would make the system that George Orwell depicted in his famous novel, '1984,' seem clumsy."

In American Stasi: Fusion Centers and Domestic Spying, Miles Kinard walks readers through some of the technologies 74 'intelligence fusion centers' use to monitor and track the daily activities of millions of Americans. This is scary, eye-opening stuff. On September 10, 2001, had a high-ranking law enforcement official told me that government agents could monitor the movements of those in possession of wireless devices in real time, absent an order from a judge, or enter a person's private residence without leaving any documentation that an entry had occurred and that private property had been seized, I would have recommended a visit to the puzzle factory.

Kinard also illustrates why the cost of America's domestic spy apparatus (estimated at $350 to $500 billion) became so outrageous. He further debunks the notion that Americans have little to fear from the newly created surveillance state as long as they have nothing to hide.

Make no mistake about it: Big Brother is here 24 hours a day, seven days a week. When it comes to liberty, ignorance is no longer bliss, which is why Miles Kinard's well researched American Stasi: Fusion Centers and Domestic Spying is a must read.

WHEN THE SHOE IS ON THE OTHER FOOT, THE DATA REVOLUTION MAKES THOSE IN BLUE CRINGE

JANUARY 15, 2012 AT 4:07 PM | FILED UNDER COP TALK

Since the attacks of September 11, 2001, the federal government has spent over $380 billion developing a nationwide surveillance network known as intelligence fusion centers.

In a previous post, When Big Brother Reaches Out and Touches, SF profiled the case of Daniel Rigmaiden—a computer hacker FBI agents located by using a state-of-the-art surveillance device that mimics a cellular telephone tower.

http://www.badgerwordsmith.com/spingolafiles/2011/09/24/when-big-brothers-stingray-technology-reaches-out-and-touches/

The methodologies of the newly created surveillance state are the focus of a soon-to-be released magazine exposé, American Stasi: Fusion Centers and Domestic Spying.

Across the nation, leaders of law enforcement agencies have heaped praise on these 'all-hazards,' multijurisdictional intelligence operations while privacy advocates warn that Big Brother is swallowing our civil liberties (see an example by clicking the below link).

http://abclocal.go.com/kgo/story?section=news/state&id=8503013

Now, however, the leaders of these same agencies find it, to say the least, unsettling that a protest organization is using some of the same technologies employed by fusion centers to target law enforcement.

On Friday, CNN reported that the group Anonymous, a clandestine organization affiliated with the Occupy Wall Street movement, is using computer technology to target police officers who use force to quell protests. Hackers have accessed law enforcement only Web sites and then posted the personal information of police officers, including their home addresses, online.

"Officers who used pepper spray on Occupy protesters," Steve Turnham and Amber Lyon report, "including NYPD Deputy Inspector Anthony Bologna and Lt. John Pike at the University of California-Davis, saw their entire life histories blasted out in Web videos and document dumps."

While the tactics of Anonymous are over the top, in the age of the Internet, virtually anyone's personal information—no matter how hard we try—is available for just a few bucks.

In his book No Place to Hide, journalist Robert O'Harrow spotlights the so-called "data revolution," where private companies, such as Acxiom, make fortunes building profiles of individual Americans for sale to marketers, insurance companies, retail outlets, as well as federal, state and local governments.

A few months ago, I learned about the data revolution, first hand, when accessing the Web site of my health care provider. In order to verify my identity, the site asked if I had ever owned one of a list of vehicles and then inquired about a relationship I maintained with a professional organization. Whether I like it or not, some company somewhere is improving its bottom line by selling my personal information.

A statement on O'Harrow's Web site sums it up well. "When you go to work, stop at the store, fly in a plane, or surf the web, you are being watched. They know where you live, the value of your home, the names of your friends and family, in some cases even what you read. Where the data revolution meets the needs of national security, there is no place to hide."

Unfortunately, law enforcement officers are no longer immune from the "data revolution," as the words "national security" can easily be interchanged with 'anyone with a credit card.'

SF READER ALERT: BE AWARE OF DNA SHARING

JANUARY 18, 2012 AT 11:59 PM | FILED UNDER CITIZEN TALK

Due to the nature of this Web site, SF receives e-mails from individuals with theories about various crimes. Sometimes, these communications do little more than pass along urban myths. Today, however, I received this e-mail from a source that I believe is creditable.

Readers interested in providing a DNA sample for determining their ancestral origins may want to think twice before doing so. At a minimum, should you decide to provide such a sample, check with the Better Business Bureau to verify that the company's business operation is ethical. Then obtain a written copy of the company's privacy statement.

* * * *

FYI—a warning for those seeking to learn more about their ancestry by submitting DNA samples to private companies that, for a fee, provide a genetic lineage.

Before submitting DNA to a third party, please take the time to read that company's privacy policy. DNA is an extremely valuable tool that data collection services could sell to insurance companies, as well as to federal, state, and local governments (many of whom purchase data from private sector entities).

When time permits, please visit this link from the Electronic Privacy Information Center (EPIC). The section entitled "Information and Background" gives some details about a company called "ChoicePoint."

http://epic.org/privacy/choicepoint/

ChoicePoint is in the data collection business. According to a filing with the Securities and Exchange Commission, one of the products they sell is "DNA identification services."

Besides allowing law enforcement agencies to link individuals to crime scenes, DNA enables health insurance companies and risk management specialists the ability to ascertain one's susceptibility to cancer, heart disease, mental illness, and a host of other health related problems.

While some might not care if a private company shares their DNA profile, the information gleaned could affect your siblings, children, and grandchildren, as they share similar DNA. Within minutes after receiving just a tad of one's personal information, data collection corporations can assemble a detailed individual dossier, which includes a list of their relatives and friends, vehicles owned, the value of your home, and an individual's net worth. As a result, traits associated with a DNA sample can easily be linked to close relatives.

Since federal law prohibits the dissemination or sale of DNA information from law enforcement databases to private entities, data collection companies rely on individuals to simply consent to providing samples by other means, which they might sell. In the world of the data mining, before providing a single detail to anyone, it is important to understand how this information is stored, used or sold.

CONVICTION IN PHOENIX BOMBING CONNECTS THE LOOSE-ENDS

FEBRUARY 25, 2012 AT 10:42 PM | FILED UNDER CONSPIRACY

On Friday, a Phoenix, Arizona jury convicted white supremacist Dennis Mahon of using an improvised explosive device to target City of Scottsdale Diversity Director Don Logan, who is African-American.[1]

In 2004, a co-worker brought a package addressed to Logan into his City of Scottsdale office. Since the package's return address listed the Arizona State Retirement System, of which the addressee is a member, Logan testified that he believed the package was a gift. After using a scissors to open the package, Logan reached inside, at which time he heard a "pop." A pipe bomb inside exploded, causing the room to fill with smoke and expended shrapnel. Logan ran into an adjacent room to find his arm severely injured.[2]

The case against Mahon was solidified when a Bureau of Alcohol, Tobacco, Firearms and Explosives (BATF) informant moved into a government-supplied mobile home located in the same trailer park where Mahon resided. The woman, 41-year-old Rebecca Williams, gained Mahon's confidence over time by sending the white supremacist racy photographs, including one depicting the former stripper in a bikini with a grenade strapped between her breasts. During one taped conversation with Mahon, Williams asked if a bomb he made ever exploded. Mahon replied, "...diversity director."[3]

Mahon's conviction in the Phoenix bombing spotlights the controversy behind his connection to a shady encampment in Adair County, Oklahoma. Named "Elohim City"—Hebrew for the word God—by its founder Robert G. Miller, this private community has distinct links to the Christian Identity movement.[4] Days before his April 19, 1995 bombing of the Alfred E. Murrah Federal Building in Oklahoma City, Timothy McVeigh telephoned Elohim City looking for Adreas Strassmeir, a former German solider, in an effort to secure a potential hideout.[5] At the time, Strassmeir was friends with Dennis Mahon and also the roommate of Michael Brescia, who investigators believed was a strong "John Doe #2" candidate in the Murrah building bombing. ATF informant Carol Howe, who had infiltrated Elohim City, told federal investigators that two other men, besides McVeigh, who visited the compound, spoke about an attack against a federal building.[6]

Prior to the Oklahoma City bombing, McVeigh used the alias Timothy Tuttle. In the fall of 1994, while at Mahon's home near Elohim City, Howe was present when Mahon allegedly received a call from Tim Tuttle.[7]

Dennis Mahon is also closely connected to Tom Metzger, the founder of the White Aryan Resistance (WAR). "ATF spokespersons confirmed that the search of Metzger's home was connected to the investigation of the 2004 bombing," said a report from the Southern Poverty Law Center. "Metzger was not arrested."[8]

The activities of loan wolf terrorists, some of whom are linked to white supremacist organizations, are, some believe, the impetus, behind section 1021 of the National Defense Authorization Act of 2012 (NDOA), which congressman and U.S. Presidential candidate Ron Paul notes, "provides for the possibility of the U.S. military acting as a kind of police force on U.S. soil, apprehending terror suspects, including Americans, and whisking them off to an undisclosed location indefinitely."[9]

The Oklahoma City and Phoenix bombings, as well as those of the eco-motivated Unabomber, Ted Kaczynski, paint a picture of domestic terrorists as brazen as our foreign enemies. Yet it will be interesting to see how the powers given to the president under the NDOA fair in a court of law, where legislation should, according to the U.S. Constitution, meet the due process requirements set forth in the Bill of Rights.

---

[1] Meyers, Amanada L. "Dennis Mahon Guilty and Daniel Mahon Acquitted in White Supremacist Bombing Trial." Huffingtonpost.com. February 25, 2012. 25 Feb. 2012. http://www.huffingtonpost.com/2012/02/25/dennis-mahon-guilty_n_1300915.html

[2] Meyers, Amanda L. "Victim of Ariz. Bombing Gives Emotional Testimony." February 1, 2012. 25 Feb. 2012. http://www.huffingtonpost.com/2012/02/25/dennis-mahon-guilty_n_1300915.html

[3] White Supremacist Convicted of Phoenix Bomb Attack. Dailymail.co.uk. February 25, 2012. 25 Feb. 2012. http://www.dailymail.co.uk/news/article-2106343/Dennis-Mahon-trial-White-supremacist-convicted-Phoenix-bomb-attack.html?ito=feeds-newsxml

[4] Shook, S., Delano, W. & Balch, W. Elohim City: a Participant-Observer Study of a Christian Identity Community. Nova Religion.

[5] Michel, L. & Herbeck, D. American Terrorist: Timothy McVeigh & the Oklahoma City Bombing. New York, NY. Regan Books, 2001.

[6] Jones S. & Israel, P. Others Unknown: Timothy McVeigh and the Oklahoma City Bombing Conspiracy.New York, NY. Perseus Books, 1998.

[7] "Where there More OKC Conspirators? The Elohim City Connection." Law2.umkc.edu. 25 Feb. 2012. http://law2.umkc.edu/faculty/projects/ftrials/mcveigh/moreconspirators.html

[8] "Neo-Nazis Arrested in Mail Bombing." Splc.org. Winter 2009. 25 Feb. 2012. http://www.splcenter.org/get-informed/intelligence-report/browse-all-issues/2009/winter/domestic-terrorism-0

[9] Gubbe, Richard S. "Editorial: Ron Paul Speaks Out, wants to Repeal Part of Defense Authorization Act." Rockrivertimes.com. February 1, 2012. 25 Feb. 2012. http://rockrivertimes.com/2012/02/01/editorial-ron-paul-speaks-out-wants-to-repeal-part-of-defense-authorization-act/

ONE WOMAN'S WILLINGNESS TO STAND-UP TO ORWELLIAN ID ACT

FEBRUARY 4, 2012 AT 3:35 PM | FILED UNDER THE COURTS

When Oklahoma native Kaye Beach sought to renew her driver's license, she refused to comply with that state's version of the Real ID Law.

In Oklahoma, and throughout 26 other states, including Wisconsin, the one digital photo taken at the counter will no longer suffice. Instead, applicants are required to submit to several photos, including a full body profile.

When Ms. Beach declined to acquiesce to the new array of photographs, officials from Oklahoma's version of the Department of Motor Vehicles denied the renewal of her driver's license. Predictably, a time came when Ms. Beach had a traffic related law enforcement contact, at which time she was cited for driving without a valid operator's license.

But instead of simply walking like a sheep to the slaughter to renew her permit, Ms. Beach fought to have her citation dismissed and then filed a lawsuit challenging the constitutionality of Oklahoma's Real ID law.

Why is Kaye Beach making such a fuss? After all, what is so difficult about submitting to a series of photographs?

The devil, of course, is in the details, as the photographs obtained by the Department of Transportation will no longer remain securely housed in a state's data base.

In late December, Milwaukee Journal Sentinel reporter Jason Stein wrote a hear no evil, see no evil article regarding Wisconsin's version of the federal Photo ID Law, which, ironically, was authored by Congressman F. James Sensenbrenner.

In the article, Stein mentions that a series of photos of each applicant will be hidden within the license and observed only with ultraviolet light. These photographs and the applicable information will then be dispatched to a private "contractor in California."

In reality, however, these photographs will be used to create a biometric image of each driver's license or ID card holder. Biometrics is the science used to design facial recognition software.

As SF mentioned in its review of Miles Kinard's magazine exposé, American Stasi: Fusion Centers and Domestic Spying, since the attacks of 9/11, the federal government has created 74 fusion centers, all of which have access to driver's license data bases.

With access to these new biometric photographs, fusion center operatives will be able to catch an image of a person on a simple CCTV camera and instantaneously determine their identity. For example, as an individual attending a Marquette basketball game is captured by a facial recognition camera at Milwaukee's Bradley Center, a computer will scan their images against a variety of data bases and mark the image; thereby, showing that a known person was at a specific location at a particular date and time.

In other words, the Real ID law creates a national identification card that government agents can access without the permit holder's consent absent a reasonable suspicion of wrong doing.

Throughout the United States, unless a party is operating a motor vehicle, individuals are not required to identify themselves to law enforcement absent a reasonable suspicion (in Wisconsin, if a party is not driving, a person is not required to identify themselves to law enforcement even if officers have a reasonable suspicion).

In a rebellion against this federal legislation, 24 states have opted out of the federal government's Real ID law, but not Wisconsin or Oklahoma.

In Wisconsin, however, residents will have the option of using the current ID system; however, if those choosing the current ID wish to travel by air or enter a federal courthouse, they will need a valid passport to do so. A hunch tells me that that DOT employees will conveniently avoid telling those at that the counter that they can opt out if they have a valid passport.

Granted, while the technology exists to invade the privacy of Americans, members of the public can demand that these intrusive methods be highly regulated or simply banned. In 1928, the U.S. Supreme Court determined that wiretapping was perfectly legal. This ruling, however, created a collective outrage with voters, who demanded changes. Six years later, congress passed the Communications Act of 1934 that banned wiretapping absent a court order.

Outrage is what it will take to stop the new Orwellian ID law.

Note: In March 2012, Wisconsin began issuing Real ID complaint identification.

OLD SCHOOL SLEUTHS WEIGH-IN ON MOST CURRENT CROP OF DETECTIVES

MARCH 31, 2012 AT 4:55 PM | FILED UNDER COP TALK

In every occupation, there is a time for reflection as those from the old school evaluate their new school practitioners. Law enforcement is no different. Make no mistake about it a pronounced generation gap exists between post-Vietnam War investigators—those who began their policing careers between 1975 to 1979—and today's current batch of Generation X and Y sleuths.

Most old school cops will grudgingly admit that today's detectives—those promoted within the last five years—are better educated and work smarter. Out of the other side of their mouths, however, post-Vietnam investigators, many of whom are now retired, take Gen X and Y detectives to task for a perceived lack of social skills. Some theorize that the computerized, social network society reduces the physical communication skills needed to read things like body language, which is important to obtain confessions.

Moreover, many post-Vietnam types believe today's detectives rely too heavily on technology to solve complex cases.

"No matter what they learn sitting in front of a computer monitor," one crusty retired detective recently told me, "a confession isn't going to simply materialize on that screen."

Without a doubt, today's investigators are armed with a wide range of technologies that, just 15-year-ago, were fodder for science fiction novels. Within a matter of minutes, operatives at federally subsidized 'intelligence fusion' centers can create a dossier on 98 percent of adult Americans, track the movements of those with cellular devices in real time, use infrared cameras to literally unmask hold-up men, and identify individuals captured on CCTV cameras through facial recognition software. These cameras are literally everywhere—mounted at the top of traffic control poles at busy intersections, on the roof tops of buildings, and inside of many private sector businesses. Advances in DNA technology enable law enforcement to easily include or exclude potential suspects from complicated crime scenes.

Author Miles Kinard profiles a vast array of new law enforcement technologies in his recently released magazine exposé, American Stasi: Fusion Centers and Domestic Spying.

Yet many old school cops argue that these technological advances have done little to increase clearance rates for major crimes.

For example, consider the homicide clearance rate in Milwaukee County. From 1990 – 1999, prior to the significant advances in DNA testing and the construction of post-9/11 intelligence fusion centers, 84 percent of Milwaukee County homicides were counted as cleared. However, from 2000 – 2008, Milwaukee County's homicide clearance rate fell to 72 percent, even as the average number of homicides declined almost 22 percent. [1]

In Dane County, which typically averages fewer than ten homicides a year, the clearance rate from 2000 – 2008 was down four percent from where it was from 1980 – 1999, even though the number of sworn law enforcement officers has significantly increased.[2]

The city of Madison is home to two of Wisconsin's highly profiled unsolved slayings, both involving college-aged co-eds. Last observed alive on State Street, 22-year-old Kelly Nolan's body was discovered in a town of Oregon field in 2007. Less than a year later, 21-year-old UW-Madison student Brittany Zimmermann was murdered by an intruder inside her Doty Street apartment.

Reading between the lines, one can almost detect the desperation in the comments of Madison Police Chief Noble Wray, a supporter of Wisconsin State Senate Bill 214 (SB-214), which would empower law enforcement to compel DNA samples from individuals simply arrested—not convicted or even charged—for a felony. [3]

Most experienced homicide investigators would likely concur that someone in Madison probably knows who killed Kelly Nolan and/or Brittany Zimmermann. The suspects likely spoke to someone in confidence. If not, friends, relatives, or neighbors might have a hunch that they know the perpetrators.

Post-Vietnam investigators might make a case that Wray's department is too intent on simply expanding the DNA pool and, instead, should focus on doing some old school police work—talking to informants; interviewing those arrested for serious offenses who might be willing to work a deal; searching for new information that enhances investigative timelines, as both of these suspects remain at-large to kill again.

Many old school investigators, including myself, will argue that new technologies—while incredibly valuable—are over relied upon by Gen X and Y detectives. In the interim, the reaction of high-ranking law enforcement administrators is to ask the legislature to encroach on the civil liberties of the populous to compensate for their investigators' willingness to wait on results from the crime lab.

As one former post-Vietnam detective recently told me, "Not too many killers are going to confess on Facebook or Twitter. You got to out there, shake the bushes, and know how to talk to people."

---

[1] "Murder Mysteries: National Statistics." KnoxvilleNews.com. 31 March 2012. http://www.knoxnews.com/data/murder-knoxville-nation/

[2] "Murder Mysteries: National Statistics." KnoxvilleNews.com. 31 March 2012. http://www.knoxnews.com/data/murder-knoxville-nation/

[3] Hogue, B. "DNA Collection Bill Proposed." Wrn.com. March 2, 2012. 31 March 2012. http://www.wrn.com/2012/03/dna-collection-bill-proposed/

LIBERTY ACTIVISTS DOING THE JOB THE MEDIA USED TO DO

MARCH 17, 2012 AT 4:19 PM | FILED UNDER CITIZEN TALK

On Friday, I had the pleasure to appear on AxXiom for Liberty, an Internet-based radio program hosted by libertarian activist Kaye Beach. Our conversation focused on the state of privacy in the United States.[1]

Last summer, as the contents of the National Defense Authorization Act (NDAA) of 2012 slowly saw the light of day, SF began turning its attention to the burgeoning American surveillance state that threatens individual autonomy. Title X, subtitle D, subsections 1021 and 1022 of the NDAA, enables authorities from the military and/or federal law enforcement to apprehend American citizens inside the U.S. or elsewhere, and then hold them indefinitely, absent due process rights, if federal authorities believe they pose a threat to the national security of the United States.[2]

One need not be a lawyer to ascertain that the NDAA conveniently ignores the Fifth and Sixth Amendments to the Bill of Rights.

Back to my appearance on AxXiom for Liberty, where Ms. Beach and I discussed a new magazine exposé, American Stasi: Fusion Centers and Domestic Spying. Author Miles Kinard describes some of the technologies used by the government to monitor the lives of ordinary American citizens. Kinard further notes that section 213 of the USA Patriot Act enables federal agents to obtain a simple letter from a supervisor—not a search warrant signed by a judge—to secretly enter and search a private residence.[3]

"Wow, this guy's [Miles Kinard] really knocked it out of the park," Kaye Beach remarked.

When executing a so-called 'sneak-and-peek' search, agents are not required to leave any notice and can seize any private property deemed "reasonably necessary;" thereby, bypassing the Fourth Amendment's requirement that a neutral and detached magistrate first issue a search warrant that specifically describes the objects of the search and the items to be seized.

If these broad, seemingly, unconstitutional rules applied to suspected terrorists, it might be easy to look the other way. Instead, the federal government is using the USA Patriot Act to target drug dealers and other common criminals.

From 2006 – 2009, federal agents used National Security letters—signed not by a judge but by an FBI supervisor—to conduct 1755 'sneak-and-peek' searches. Only 15 of these entries—just .85 percent—targeted suspected terrorists, while over 92 percent were for evidence of drug trafficking.[4] In other words, the USA Patriot Act's provisions allowing warrantless searches of private residences has enabled federal law enforcement to usurp the Fourth Amendment.

Common sense and a respect for the Bill of Rights dictates that if targets of 'sneak-and-peek' searches do not meet the criteria of terror suspects, congress needs to prohibit such searches. Lawmakers further need to hold those authorizing these searches accountable if the USA Patriot Act's provisions serve as little more than a catalyst to operate outside the bounds of the Fourth Amendment for convenience sake.

Having a dialog about these issues is important, even though a majority of federal lawmakers—in both political parties—seem disinterested. Activists, such as Kaye Beach and her fellow libertarians, serve as government watchdogs, while, at the same time, it appears, the mainstream media is content on turning a blind-eye to matters such as Orwellian biometric identification, the intricacies of the NDAA, and the use of facial recognition software that enables agents to identify Americans from social network photographs and/or CCTV.

On the other hand, the popularity of presidential candidate Ron Paul in the 18 to 30-year-old demographic should serve as a wake-up call for big government Republican Party elites. An ever-growing group of Americans increasingly sees the federal government as an obese 800-pound man gobbling-up financial resources and individual freedoms; whereby, the only way to save him is shrinking his scope and size via a calorie restrictive, revenue starvation diet.

<u>UPDATE</u>: Kentucky Senator Rand Paul asks Virginia's Governor to sign a bill prohibiting that state's law enforcement agencies from assisting the U.S. military's detention of Americans absent due process.

---

[1] Beach, K. "Friday, March 16, 6 to 8 p.m. CST, AxXiom for Liberty Live. Guest, Former Homicide Detective, Author Steve Spingola." http://axiomamuse.wordpress.com/2012/03/16/friday-march-16-6-8-pm-cst-axxiom-for-liberty-live-guest-former-homicide-detective-author-steven-spingola/

[2] Knickerbocker, B. "Guantanamo for U.S. Citizens? Senate Bill Raises

Questions." www.csmonitor.com. December 3, 2011. 16 March 2012. http://www.csmonitor.com/USA/Justice/2011/1203/Guantanamo-for-US-citizens-Senate-bill-raises-questions

[3] Kinard, M. American Stasi: Fusion Centers and Domestic Spying. Badger Wordsmith, LLC. Wales, WI. 2012.

[4] Walker, J. "What Cases have the Patriot Act's Sneak-and-Peek Warrants been used for?" www.reason.com. September 7, 2011. 16 March 2012. http://reason.com/blog/2011/09/07/what-cases-have-the-patriot-act

SECURITY VS. PRIVACY: AN INTERVIEW WITH WUWM

APRIL 18, 2012 AT 10:21 PM | FILED UNDER MEDIA INTERVIEWS

Yesterday, WUWM aired an interview I did with Lake Effect's Stephanie Lecci regarding America's post-9/11 surveillance state. We discussed the use of drones, the expansion of intelligence fusion centers, infrared technology, the spread of facial recognition software, as well as the ever-evolving state of the law pertaining to surveillance.

To hear the interview, please visit the following link:

http://www.wuwm.com/programs/lake_effect/lake_effect_segment.php?segmentid=9105

THE NEW 'MARK OF THE BEAST' HAS INVESTIGATORS LOVIN' IT

APRIL 14, 2012 AT 3:29 PM | FILED UNDER CITIZEN TALK

Earlier last week, Milwaukee talk-radio host Jay Weber discussed Gov. Scott Walker's support of a bill to collect DNA when a person is simply booked—not convicted or even charged—for a felony offense.

One of the callers to Weber's show, who opposed the bill, cited the movie Minority Report—a film featuring a futuristic group of investigators charged with apprehending suspects based on an 'foreknowledge' of their crimes. The same caller also noted that—like the 'mark of the beast'—the government might someday require the installation of tracking devices in all new born children.

The "mark of the beast" is, of course, a reference to the Book of Revelations, Chapter 13 versus 16-18, which reads:

"And he causeth all, both small and great, rich and poor, free and bond, to receive a mark in their right hand, or in their foreheads and that no man might buy or sell, save he that had the mark, or the name of the beast, or the number of his name. Here is wisdom. Let him that hath understanding count the number of the beast: for it is the number of a man; and his number is Six hundred threescore and six (i.e. 666)."

In a sense, the government no longer needs to install tracking devices in newborns. In today's America, most parents provide such tracking devices, called cellular telephones, to their children at early ages. As of September 2010, eighty-two percent of adult Americans owned a cellular telephone.

Seizing upon the opportunity to monitor, locate, and identify potential suspects, federal, state and local law enforcement agencies routinely use cellular technology against its users.

A high-profile hit-and-run case from the Twin Cities highlights the role cellular tracking technology plays in criminal investigations.

On August 23, 2011, at about 11:10 p.m., Amy Senser, 45, the wife of former Minnesota Viking Joe Senser, was en route to pick-up her daughter from a Katy Perry concert in downtown St. Paul. The criminal complaint alleges that as Mrs. Senser took an exit ramp off the interstate she struck and killed 38-year-old Anousone Phanthavong, who was standing outside his stalled vehicle in a construction zone. The impact knocked Phathavong nearly 40 feet. Prosecutors allege and Senser's defense concedes that she left the scene. The next day, Senser's attorney contacted the authorities to report the accident, although he alleges that his client did not stop because she did not believe she had struck a person—a defense under Minnesota law.

But it did not take long for investigators to hone in on their target's cellular telephone data.

Amy Senser's phone records show that she called her daughter at 11:08 p.m.—two minutes prior to Phathavong being struck—and was talking on the telephone when the accident likely occurred. Investigators further subpoenaed tower data from Sensor's cellular provider, which, prosecutors claim, indicates that the woman drove around for nearly an hour after the accident.

While prosecutors have not charged Amy Sensor with any alcohol violations, her attorneys have filed a motion to "bar prosecutors from asking witnesses about Senser's drinking habits or using any "testimony about impairment, DWI references or other testimony that Defendant was under the influence of alcohol or drugs" on the night of the crash."

http://www.twincities.com/localnews/ci_20390139/amy-senser-hit-run-case-she-was-cellphone

Nonetheless, prosecutors believe that Amy Sensor's cellular telephone records paint a portrait of panicked driver.

And, of course, even if a conscientious cellular telephone user turns off their GPS location finder, the data stored on the computer of a cellular provider triangulates a device's location between towers. This information is generally stored for up to a year. Some privacy advocates claim the only way to avoid tracking is to turn a cellular telephone off and to store the computer—because that is what a cellular telephone really is—in the trunk of a vehicle when traveling.

If the 'mark of the beast,' as mentioned in the Book of Revelations, is a tracking device found in an individual's right hand, then 90 percent of cellular telephone users, including myself, have been tagged.

In the interim, while the concepts portrayed in the movie Minority Report are likely decades away, for those who believe that freedom equals an expectation of at least some level of privacy, that movie's sequel, Majority Report—where we are all followed, and our thoughts duly noted via smartphone apps, electronic transactions, and Internet usage—is, unfortunately, now playing everywhere.

LAPDOGS: THE MEDIA AND THE SURVEILLANCE STATE

MAY 13, 2012 AT 4:33 PM | FILED UNDER CITIZEN TALK

It is no secret that since the horrific events of September 11, 2001, large corporations have teamed-up with their K Street lobbyists and willing members of congress to construct an American surveillance state.

Unfortunately, Americans seem more concerned with the finalists on Survivor or Snooki's latest meltdown than the incremental creation of a technological iron curtain that rivals that of China.

The same can be said about the majority of the American mainstream media—the so-called Fourth Estate. It wasn't long ago that television news magazines, such as 60 Minutes, kept a watchful eye on overzealous politicians and government bureaucrats.

In 2012, however, local television news wastes its resources searching for dirty restaurant kitchens or standing in the middle of a blizzard reporting the obvious—that it is snowing outside—than keeping tabs on state and local governments.

And the Milwaukee Journal Sentinel, well, sadly, they're more concerned about the contents of plastic or winning Pulitzer Prizes for bashing one of the few institutions in town that actually performs well (the Milwaukee Police Department) than the civil liberties of the citizenry.

Many would argue that, when it comes to the development of a virtual surveillance state, the American mainstream media is more of a lapdog than a watchdog.

There are some exceptions. Washington Post reporters Dana Priest and William Arkin's series Top Secret America documents the expansive nature of domestic surveillance. Some in the know believe the cost could exceed $350 billion.

Other organizations, such as the Electronic Privacy Information Center (EPIC) and the Rutherford Institute, have challenged the federal government's anti-transparency agenda championed by both Republicans and Democrats, many of whom receive campaign contributions from political action committees and/or individuals affiliated with the new security-industrial complex.

Late last week, the Washington Post reported that a federal appeals court denied a request from EPIC (www.epic.org) to see communications between Google and the National Security Agency (NSA).

At the same time, many local law enforcement agencies are using or are preparing to use biometric iris scanners to identify individuals. Police officers can now use an app on an I-Phone to scan a human iris.

And in Leone, Mexico, iris scan experimentation is being conducted with the hopes of importing this technology for even broader use in the United States.

http://www.youtube.com/watch?v=avCEEVPWHRU

Thousands of corporations, such as Lockheed Martin, strand to profit by developing the apparatus needed to capture and catalog the daily activities of law-abiding Americans. While big brother advocates point to security as their goal, the information gathered by surveillance state might be used to quell public discourse.

Just ask 'Joe the Plumber' about information from government databases being used against those who dare challenge a politician.

Meanwhile, what is the headline in today's Sunday paper? That some of the income generated by executives of private companies might not get fully reported. Go figure.

MADISON'S CURMUDGEON MAYOR SEEKS TO END AN ERA HE CREATED

MAY 6, 2012 AT 5:58 AM | FILED UNDER CITIZEN TALK

For the last 43 years, Madison, Wisconsin has hosted the Mifflin Street block party in early spring. What started as a drunken, dope-smoking protest against the Vietnam War has morphed into a pretext to get intoxicated and blow-off some steam prior the start of final exams week.

In 1969, Madison's current mayor, Paul Soglin, represented the Eighth Ward on that city's Common Council. Arrested twice during Mifflin's inaugural debauchery, Soglin, now 67, serves as an example of an aging radical turned curmudgeon.

Like the block party's original participants, today's Mifflin Street attendees consume alcohol to excess, thumb their noses at law enforcement, and make casual observers wonder if this 20-something generation lacks a basic moral compass.

In other words, little has changed, although one could argue that the old cliché 'meet the new boss, same as the old boss' rings ironic, as the 24-year-old, 1969 Paul Soglin probably never envisioned himself as the establishment figure in-charge of the block party's ultimate demise.

After the 2011 Mifflin Street block party—marred by the outrageous conduct of a handful of out-of-control hooligans—Soglin sounded the alarm to end the event.

"Some students," wrote New York Times reporter Drik Johnson, "say their mayor is suffering from an affliction that might be called "baby boomer amnesia," a condition that young people say is common among parents of a certain age."

In recognition of his "baby boomer amnesia" syndrome, Soglin appeared to retract some of the comments that he made post-2011 Mifflin. Instead of actually taking a stand on the issue, however, the mayor appears to favor regulating the block party out of existence.

In years past, once party goers—sometimes 10,000 strong—flooded the two-city blocks, police would close down the 400 and 500 blocks of W. Mifflin Street with barricades. City leaders now insist that the roadway remain open. Law enforcement will deal with partygoers who dare overflow into the thoroughfare with citations. Moreover, for the first time, renters and property owners can post 'no trespassing signs' on Mifflin Street dwellings; whereby, police can take action against individuals loitering or simply standing on a portion of such properties.

These rules, of course, are specifically designed to hamper the Mifflin Street event and, incrementally, regulate the block party out of existence. These new mandates mark a change in Soglin's status from aging-hippie/old-fart to Madison's party-crippling Czar.

Some speculate that by 2015 the Mifflin Street block party will be verboten.

Unfortunately, this year's 2012 event has snared celebrity causality—University of Wisconsin tailback Montee Ball, who, in the 2011 season, tied Barry Sanders' all-time NCAA Division I record by scoring 39 touchdowns in a single season. Some college football prognosticators list Ball as the leading candidate for this year's Heisman Trophy.

What dastardly deed did Ball allegedly commit in a city that once prided itself as a proponent of civil liberties? He had the gall to stand on a porch, knowingly or unknowingly, where a property owner had posted a 'no trespassing' sign.

The Milwaukee Journal Sentinel and WTMJ radio and television sports reporter Trenni Kusnierek quickly relayed the details. In many instances, the JS and WTMJ refuse to identify an individual until they are charged with an offense. However, the saga of a star athlete being in the wrong place at the wrong time was apparently too juicy to pass-up on a slow news weekend.

In the future, Montee might choose to play hard-Ball—pun intended—with news outlets too willing to report something that is really not newsworthy. SF suggests that Ball refuse to provide interviews and/or sound bites to news gathers too intent on making a mountain out of a molehill.

And Ball probably is not the only student to get caught in the tangled web weaved by Madison's grumpy-old mayor who, in his golden years, suddenly favors "a sense of order." As the 'do as I say, not as I do' generation of hippies slowly sets-sail for the geriatric ward, karma is not a concept they apparently contemplate.

DRONES AND THE JUDGE

JUNE 8, 2012 AT 3:56 AM | FILED UNDER COP TALK

In the forefront of the debate on security vs. privacy is the use of drones over American airspace. UAVs—a government euphemism for un-manned aircraft—might be as small as a golf ball or as large as a small jet. Some of these hovering vehicles are disguised as hummingbirds or insects.

http://newsfeed.time.com/2011/02/17/bird-bond-new-nano-hummingbird-camera-takes-spying-to-the-sky/

Drones have infrared capabilities, which enable them to see through the walls of your home or office. These machines also contain high-resolution cameras to record and store data. Downloaded to a mainframe computer, photographs and other biometrical information are stored forever.

In Thursday's Washington Times, former New Jersey judge and Fox News contributor Andrew Napolitano describes the intrusive capabilities of drones and illustrates how these golf-ball sized machines will literally shatter the concept of privacy in America.

http://www.washingtontimes.com/news/2012/jun/7/big-brothers-all-seeing-eye/

Judge Napolitano's article comes on the heels of a Wired Magazine exposé by James Bamford—one of the world's foremost experts on the federal government's $2 billion electronic eavesdropping initiative.

http://www.wired.com/threatlevel/2012/03/ff_nsadatacenter/all/1

In the comments section of Bamford's article, Mark Newell—a name that might be familiar to some of you—notes:

"Not very long ago..... I actually believed that I would be willing to sacrifice a bit of freedom for security. I believed that a guard or cop at the entrance to my community, checking I.D. would be better than carloads of gang members roaming through creating havoc. I once laughed at those who mistrusted the government and prepared for survival, should things go sideways. I supported efforts by our so-called "leaders" to monitor society, in search for the ever present evil. Not long ago.....I slept.

"Anyone who really believes that the simple act of discussing this on the internet has not steered electronic ears in your direction….is sound asleep and I understand that. Someone alluded to it and I repeat this truth. In 1935 Germany... many citizens felt uneasy and sensed that doom was on the way. More laughed such talk off and continued to find reasons to smile and enjoy the day. We all know the end of that story.

"The new I Pad was released!!!!! Snooky had a meltdown! My Mac Pro is awesome!!! These trinkets that keep us giggling and focused on nothing.... this addiction to instant gratification…….. this will be our downfall.

"There's a storm brewing."

MAJORITY REPORT: IS THE ELECTRONIC IRON CURTAIN CALL UPON US?

JUNE 17, 2012 AT 3:12 AM | FILED UNDER CONSPIRACY

On occasion, I run into people who ask why the Spingola Files (SF) is concerned about the explosive growth of private corporations that make millions of dollars selling high tech surveillance equipment or privately collected information to the federal government and/or local law enforcement agencies.

Many of those who ask do not understand the scope and depth of data collected and stored on individual Americans. Privacy advocate Miles Kinard reports that several private sector companies can, on demand, sell dossiers on 98 percent of all adult Americans to the local, state or federal law enforcement agencies. This information includes individual assets, personal health information, travel locations, hotel reservations, vehicle rental data, Internet usage, and entertainment purchases.

By procuring data from private entities, intelligence fusion centers are able to work around laws that prohibit government agents from collecting information on Americans absent a reasonable suspicion, as the USA Patriot Act winks-and-nods when its own officials simply purchase these dossiers.

Liberty activist Kaye Beach—the host of the blog and radio program Axxiom for Liberty—recently sent an alert regarding a new member of the ever expanding security-industrial complex.

http://axiomamuse.wordpress.com/2012/06/16/are-oklahoma-cops-using-spy-cams-to-become-super-snoopers/

The private company Vigilant Video (VV) is a prime example of what occurs when free-flowing government money meets those seeking to make a buck by satisfying big brother's ever growing appetite. A VV software program called "Line-up," catalogs "all human face events into a centralized database." Facial recognition software then enables users—primarily government agencies—to receive real time alerts anytime a person of interest is captured on video.

This type of turnkey totalitarian technology breathes life into the scary world portrayed in the movie Minority Report, where police departments employ agents known as "precogs" that seize alleged criminals based only on an 'foreknowledge' of possible crimes.

And while our federal representatives stuff their campaign coffers with security-industrial complex PAC money or funds contributed by their hired guns at K Street lobbying firms, one has to wonder if congress is on the verge of signing-off on an electronic iron curtain—a place where every book we purchase, each text message we send, and every page we surf on the Internet, is neatly cataloged and stored?

Former New Jersey judge and Fox News analyst Andrew Napolitano comments on these matters in a blog post at Reason Magazine. Over the course of the past year, Napolitano's rhetoric has become increasingly heated as, in his opinion, freedom, as we know it, is vanishing at light speed.

It is time to demand—not ask—that our elected representatives protect the privacy of Americans by refusing to purchase our private information from for profit businesses all too willing to feed the beast.

DO-GOODER SIGNS PROVIDE SOLACE FOR ACTIVE SHOOTERS

JULY 21, 2012 AT 3:34 PM | FILED UNDER HOMICIDE

Almost three years ago, retired Milwaukee Police Department Sergeant Mike Kuspa and I formed the Spingola Group (SG)—a consulting service that focuses on improving an organization's response before, during, and after a critical incident. At SG, instructors provide real world instruction to academic institutions and private businesses based not on perception but reality.

http://badgerwordsmith.com/spingolagroup/

And it was reality that hit home on early Friday morning that resulted in the tragic shooting deaths of a dozen people—dubbed, by some, the massacre and the midnight matinee, in Aurora, Colorado—that graphically illustrates how just one psychologically fragile human being can devastate an entire community.

In the immediate aftermath of the multiple shooting deaths, the finger pointing has already begun. America's busybody, elitist mayor, New York City's Michael Bloomberg, is calling for more gun control.

"I mean, there are so many murders with guns every day," Bloomberg told the Village Voice, "it's just got to stop."

But the Americans who actually walk the streets, recreate in parks, and use public transit know better.

The United States government, with all its surveillance equipment, eavesdropping capabilities, and well-paid federal agents, prevents only a small portion of illegal drugs from entering our country. Guns—even if an outright ban existed—will still be present, but only the nefarious among us will violate the law to procure, sell, and carry them.

In the Milwaukee area, Marcus Theaters has signs posted that prohibit those with concealed carried permits from bringing firearms onto their properties.

These are the same signs that James Holmes—the shooter at the Aurora, Colorado theater—likely ignored. After all, reality dictates that do-gooder, no carry policies do little more than provide killers, like Holmes, with some solace in knowing that their law-abiding victims have voluntarily disarmed.

Reality dictates that, from time-to-time, troubled individuals will commit evil acts when they encounter troubling times. Some mental health experts believe that many of those who commit suicide act on impulse as a cloud of intense depression—one that might pass with time—descends upon them.

Signs prohibiting firearms do not deter troubled persons like James Holmes. An active shooter's goal is to take as many lives as possible. The perpetrators of these senseless acts have little to fear from signs or law enforcement, as they often anticipate taking their own lives.

Yet one has to wonder how many Colorado concealed carry permit holders left their firearms in the trunks of their cars in the theater's parking lot while Holmes sprayed the innocents with bullets?

DEMANDS FOR CELL PHONE RECORDS SHOW BIG BROTHER IS WATCHING

JULY 14, 2012 AT 7:05 AM | FILED UNDER CITIZEN TALK

Over the course of the last decade, law enforcement officers have come to appreciate the significance of cellular telephone technology as a method for tracking Americans after-the-fact or in real time.

In an April 14 post, SF discussed a Twin Cities criminal case where investigators used cellular telephone technology to ascertain the movements of Amy Senser—the wife of former Minnesota Viking Joe Senser—just prior to and after a fatal traffic accident.

On Monday, the New York Times noted that, in 2011 alone, law enforcement agencies inundated cellular telephone carriers with 1.3 million demands "seeking text messages, caller locations and other information in the course of investigations."

One company alone, Sprint, receives 1,500 demands each day from investigative agencies seeking to use cellular telephone data for surveillance purposes.

http://markey.house.gov/content/letters-mobile-carriers-reagrding-use-cell-phone-tracking-law-enforcement

"At least one carrier," the New York Times reports, "referred some inappropriate requests [from local law enforcement] to the FBI."

Data compiled by The Pew Research Center indicates that 83 percent of Americans (just over 207 million individuals) own cellular telephones, which means, in 2011, police sought access to the records of one of every 159 Americans with a mobile device.

http://pewinternet.org/Reports/2011/Cell-Phones.aspx

One of the big brother organizations in favor of increasing the use of cellular surveillance is the International Association of Chiefs of Police (IACP). In the U.S. alone, this group has lobbied for and received $647 million in federal grants for local law enforcement in the upcoming fiscal year alone, even though our national government is expected to run-up another trillion dollars in new debt.

Local law enforcement agencies use a significant portion of these funds to purchase invasive technologies—such as automatic license plate readers and software that enables national "information sharing" initiatives—that conduct surveillance and monitor the movements of all Americans absent a reasonable suspicion of any criminal wrongdoing.

Fusion centers have software that has the ability to track individual movements within buildings and dwellings, room-by-room, floor-by-floor.

As technology continues to evolve, Americans need to contact their federal representatives and demand that congress take measures to protect its citizens from intrusive fishing expeditions. Privacy, in a sense, is a personal choice to conceal information from others. The days of bluntly telling a busy-body, such as New York Mayor Michael Bloomberg or a statist organization like the IACP, to 'Mind your own damn business' is, unfortunately, a remnant of a bygone era.

NYC'S MAYOR AND THE BIG APPLE POLICE STATE

AUGUST 17, 2012 AT 8:28 AM | FILED UNDER CITIZEN TALK

In today's political climate, news media outlets—both mainstream and otherwise—seem more intent on distracting voters than encouraging discourse on the serious matters facing the American public.

Sure, while some key issues, such as the explosion of the federal debt ($5.1 trillion in just the last 3.5 years), an economy growing at a morbid pace, and the future of entitlement programs, will get a fair hearing, elected officials from both major political parties are winking-and-nodding at the rapid growth of government surveillance.

In fact, when it comes to invasive, taxpayer funded technology trumping individual privacy, political party identification and liberal or conservative labels are not applicable.

In a rush to duplicate the 'big brother is watching' society, the political class morphs into two camps—statist or constitutionalist. Unfortunately, since K Street lobbyists with cash to donate to campaigns represent the former, lawmakers carrying water for the over 1,900 corporations that sell their wares to governmental entities tend to rule the day.

An unabashed advocate for the all-encompassing police state, New York City's mayor is the portrait of the consummate statist politician. A wealthy east coast elitist, Michael Bloomberg's policies undermine the concept of individual liberty. His police department continues to use a 'stop-and-frisk' strategy that, opponents argue, ignores the constitutionally accepted standard—a reasonable suspicion—to target persons who might be armed. Bloomberg has also sought to limit the sale of soda pop, restrict access to baby formula in order to encourage mothers to breastfeed, and serves as an advocate for gun control policies that trample the Second Amendment.

One could argue that Bloomberg's political philosophy is closer to that of Russian Federation President Vladimir Putin than James Madison. In his role as a former KGB agent, Putin swore an oath to uphold he policies of the Soviet police state. Bloomberg, on the other hand, seems intent to build the infrastructure of the American surveillance state and then sell the technology to others.

In early August, Mayor Bloomberg proudly unveiled the Domain Awareness System (DAS), a computer network created by the NYPD and the Microsoft Corporation that uses information gathered from a vast array of public and private surveillance cameras, radiation detectors, license plate readers and crime reports, at a cost of $30 to $40 million.

"We can track where a car associated with a murder suspect is currently located and where it's been over the past several days, weeks or months," NYPD Police Commissioner Raymond Kelly told the New York Daily News.

In order to track potential suspects, however, DAS must monitor everyone caught on a security camera or operating a vehicle, and then store the data for retrieval.

"Bloomberg is forecasting that NYC will make back every penny they spend on Domain Awareness," a comment posted in New Yorker Magazine notes. "But who will be footing the bill for these domestic surveillance systems in other cities? The truth is the American taxpayer or, the children, grandchildren and great-grandchildren of the American taxpayer. This is just more of the money that is being flushed down the great American war on terror toilet while this once prosperous country succumbs to its own carefully cultivated hysteria and the resulting gold rush of military, defense and domestic security spending."

One can bet with the popularity of the i-Phone and i-Pad dramatically decreasing the sales of Microsoft's Windows operating systems that Bill Gates et al are looking to reach inside the big government cooking jar. Unfortunately, in this economy, where politicians pick winner and losers, the concept of the American dream has given way to those looking to feed from the statist trough.

FEDS SEIZE FORMER MARINE, EAGLE SCOUT FOR FACEBOOK POSTS

AUGUST 22, 2012 AT 10:43 PM | FILED UNDER THE COURTS

Ask anyone who has resided in a nation under authoritarian rule and they will state, unequivocally, that hell hath no fury like a police state.

As he sits in a VA psychiatric hospital, Brandon Raub, 26, a former U.S. Marine and Eagle Scout, is learning first hand that—in the era of the Patriot Act—while the First Amendment guarantees freedom of speech, it is freedom after speech that separates liberty from tyranny.

On August 16, members of the FBI, Secret Service and Chesterfield County police arrived at Raub's residence. Having inquired about his recent Facebook posts, agents seized Raub, who served tours in Iraq and Afghanistan, for a mental health evaluation.

ABC News reports that Raub's post, "Sharpen up my axe; I'm here to sever heads," appears to be the primary reason he was seized. This sentence is a quote from the lyrics of the song "Bring Me Down" by the heavy metal band Swollen Members.

"The case," writes ABC's Jason Ryan, "has pitted First Amendment freedoms against potential security concerns...At a court hearing on Monday Raub was ordered to be detained for mental evaluation for 30 days. Court records on Raub only showed traffic violations."

The Rutherford Institute—a Charlottesville, Virginia, legal foundation—is representing Raub pro bono.

"As we are learning, what is happening to Brandon Raub—arrested with no warning, targeted for doing nothing more than speaking out against the government, detained against his will, and isolated from his family, friends and attorneys—has happened many times before. These are the kinds of things that take place in totalitarian societies," said John W. Whitehead, president of The Rutherford Institute. "Any American who claims to love their country—no matter what their political leanings are—should be outraged and alarmed over the abuses being meted out by government officials and tolerated by the courts."

Federal authorities claim that Raub's comments are "terrorist in nature." This type of terminology is often times used by autocratic regimes in an attempt to marginalize opponents of the government.

The First Amendment to the Bill of Rights, which states, in part, that "Congress shall make no law...abridging the freedom of speech," allegedly protects Americans from overzealous government agents. Since the passage of the USA Patriot Act, however, rights enumerated in the First, Fourth, Fifth and Sixth Amendments of the U.S. Constitution have, sometimes, been conveniently bypassed.

Certainly, if forcibly seizing Americans against their will for posting lyrics of tasteless music qualifies as "terrorist in nature," one can only imagine how many heavy metal and rap artists will soon have their tickets to the puzzle factory punched.

Moreover, if violent lyrics are now the standard for a mental health evaluation, will the FBI investigate the members of Dead Prez, a rap group, whose lyrics to the song "Hell Yeah," read, in part:

"We gonna order take out and when we see the driver

We gonna stick the 25 up in his face......

White boy in the wrong place at the right time

Soon as the car door open up he mine

We roll up quick and put the pistol to his nose

By the look on his face he probably shitted in his clothes

You know what this is, it's a stick up

Gimme the do' from your pickups."

SF encourages its readers to voice their concerns about Raub's seizure to their federal representatives in congress.

UPDATE: CIRCUIT COURT ORDERS BRANDON RAUB'S RELEASE

AUGUST 23, 2012 AT 6:32 PM | FILED UNDER THE COURTS

Just hours ago, a circuit court judge in Virginia dismissed a detention petition filed against a former Marine and one time Eagle Scout.

Circuit Court Judge Allan Sharrett called the petition of involuntary confinement against Brandon Raub, 26, "devoid of any factual allegations that it could not be reasonably expected to give rise to a case or controversy."

Housed in a psychiatric ward since his seizure by FBI agents and Chesterfield County police on August 16, Raub's release is imminent.

"This is a great victory for the First Amendment and the rule of law," said John W. Whitehead, president of The Rutherford Institute.

The Rutherford Institute (TRI) was instrumental in providing pro bono legal assistance to Raub.

Brandon Raub's seizure against his will for expressing political opinions and posting lyrics from the heavy metal group Swollen Member on Facebook were viewed by liberty activists as akin to the tactics employed by a police state, where opponents of the government are frequently labeled terrorists or branded mentally unstable. Such was the case recently in the Russian Federation, where a band of punk rock musicians were convicted of "hooliganism" and sentenced to two years in prison.

Watch the video: **https://www.rutherford.org/multimedia/on_target/brandon_raub_and_the_thought_police/**

IS THE U.S. DEPARTMENT OF JUSTICE TARGETING THE VIEWS OF MILITARY VETERANS?

AUGUST 29, 2012 AT 10:53 PM | FILED UNDER THE COURTS

Those of us 'locals'—a term often used by the feds in reference to county and municipal law enforcement officers—who have experience dealing with the FBI, ATF, DEA, the Secret Service and ICE, know very well that federal field agents rarely, if ever, take a person into custody without running the details through their SAC (special agent in-charge). Sometimes 'local' coppers, who have affected hundreds of arrests without the blessing of a supervisor, snicker as they watch federal agents jump through the bureaucratic hoops required to take an individual into custody.

Hence, when a large group of federal agents swarm a residence, one can be fairly certain that the immediate supervisor of those involved, most likely their RAC (regional agent in-charge) and probably someone at the U.S. Justice Department, is keenly aware of what is transpiring.

This is what makes the investigation of former Marine Brandon Raub so troubling. In all likelihood, a high-ranking federal agent and/or an official at the U.S. Department of Justice signed-off on the seizure and subsequent emergency detention of the 26-year-old Virginia business owner.

Yesterday, Mr. Raub explained how the ordeal went down during an interview with The Rutherford Institute's (TRI) John Whitehead.

http://www.youtube.com/watch?v=N5dA1N3S9Es

SF discussed the seizure of the former Marine in an August 22 post.

http://www.badgerwordsmith.com/spingolafiles/2012/08/22/feds-seize-former-marine-eagle-scout-for-facebook-posts/

It appears that Raub's political beliefs (he sees the President of the United States as exercising quasi-dictatorial powers through executive orders), as well as some violent lyrics regurgitated on his Facebook page from the rock band Swollen Member, caused federal agents to take action.

Since Raub's ordeal has come-to-light, however, veterans around the country have contacted TRI to complain that former military personnel have had similar experiences.

"As we are learning, Brandon Raub is not the first veteran to be targeted for speaking out against the government, detained against his will—despite having threatened no one, and isolated from his family, friends and attorneys," Whitehead said in a news release.

Whitehead further announced that, at Brandon Raub's request, TRI plans to file a civil lawsuit regarding a wrongful detention.

Let us hope that the discovery generated from this court action shines some light on whom, specifically, approved Raub's seizure and who, if anyone, from the U.S. Justice Department signed-off on the operation.

Documents and testimony from Justice Department officials involved in Operation Fast and Furious have cast a long shadow of doubt in the halls of congress. Now our nation's veterans need to know that their colleagues—many of whom have put their lives on the line in combat—can feel free to exercise their First Amendment rights once discharged without a nameless psychiatrist, absent so much as a meaningful interview, ascertaining that their political point-of-view is somehow indicative of mental instability.

Why there are some who would say that borrowing 40 percent of what a governmental body spends is crazy, but, hey, for the sake of argument, we won't go there.

POLICE CHIEF'S ASSOCIATION LOBBIES AGAINST ANTI-BIG BROTHER LEGISLATION

SEPTEMBER 1, 2012 AT 12:41 PM | FILED UNDER CITIZEN TALK

Over the course of the past year, two criminal prosecutions have significantly raised the public's awareness of government surveillance.

On January 23, the U.S. Supreme Court handed down its decision in Jones v. the United States. In a narrowly defined opinion, the court ruled that the placement of a GPS device on a privately owned vehicle on an owner's property is a search. The majority noted, "...when the Government does engage in a physical intrusion of a constitutionally protected area in order to obtain information, that intrusion may constitute a violation of the Fourth Amendment."

In a de facto sense, the court determined that a vehicle parked on private property falls under the curtilage doctrine, even if the driveway is accessible to the public.

The Jones decision, though, does not restrict the attachment of a GPS device to a vehicle on public property. Moreover, agents can still attach a device to a vehicle on private property with a court order.

Another case with national implications emanated from a federal district court in Phoenix, where the U.S. Attorney's office prosecuted Daniel Rigmaiden on charges of conspiracy, wire fraud, and identity theft.

In order to ascertain Rigmaiden's location, FBI agents used a device called a 'Stingray,' which mimics a cellular telephone tower. Traveling in a $500,000 high-tech van, agents are able to locate a cellular signal, triangulate the machine's data from three towers, and, thereby, determine a target's whereabouts within 25 meters. Stingray technology bypasses a cellular tower's digital security absent the cellular telephone company's consent.

Reading between the lines, in the Rigmaiden case it appears that agents had obtained a National Security Letter, which is little more than a written document from an FBI supervisor that authorizes a search. Since the passage of the USA Patriot Act, certain searches, even of private residences, no longer require judicial oversight. Critics argue that permitting law enforcement agencies to authorize their own searches is akin to letting the fox guard the chicken coop.

In Rigmaiden, the district court determined that the search was Constitutional, and further denied the defense access to relevant information concerning the actual technology.

Nonetheless, the Jones and Rigmaiden cases clearly illustrate that, while technology is advancing at light speed, the laws required to regulate intrusive electronic surveillance are moving through the halls of congress and state legislatures at a snail's pace.

Things, however, are about to change. Public awareness of the surge in government surveillance, as well as the perception that the USA Patriot Act was simply a ruse to circumvent the Fourth Amendment, is causing some lawmakers to take action.

One such important piece of legislation is currently making its way through Congress. H.R. 2168, also known as the "Geolocational Privacy and Surveillance Act," is heading for a hearing before the House Subcommittee on Crime, Terrorism, and Homeland Security. This bill prohibits the interception of GPS or other cellular location data by private entities or government agents absent a search warrant.

When using cellular telephones—devices that users have paid for—Americans need to know that their privacy, absent an order from a court, is paramount.

Of course, the International Association of Chiefs of Police (IACP)—a global organization that views the American Constitution as an obstructionist document—is lobbying hard to defeat H.R. 2168.

In a letter to U.S. Rep. Lamar Smith (R-TX), ICAP President Walter McNeal wrote, "requests for search warrants cannot adopt a "one size fits all" approach and must be evaluated on a case by case basis before a decision is made for the need to establish the level of probable cause."

Mr. McNeal's comments, unfortunately, illustrate the ICAP's apparent contempt for the Fourth Amendment, as virtually every search pertaining to a criminal investigation, whether it involves a high-profile homicide or a low-level misdemeanor, is evaluated for probable cause.

If using a GPS or location finder search, similar to the technology used by the Stingray device, is required, then—absent consent or exigent circumstances—it is not unreasonable or time consuming for law enforcement agents to obtain a search warrant. Prior to the USA Patriot Act, obtaining court orders for such information was standard practice.

So it is important to get on the horn and call your member of congress and senators. Ask them to support H.R. 2168 and ignore the whiners at the ICAP.

WHY NSA IS AN ACRONYM FOR 'NEVER SAY ANYTHING'

SEPTEMBER 2, 2012 AT 2:11 PM | FILED UNDER CONSPIRACY

William Binney is a former 32-year employee of the National Security Agency (NSA), an organization that is currently in the process of constructing a $2 billion eavesdropping facility in rural Utah.

When the NSA turned its attention to reading, listening to, and storing domestic telephone conversations, e-mails, and faxes, Binney turned whistleblower.

The following is a link to a must-see article and Web video by New York Times reporter Laura Poitras:

http://www.nytimes.com/2012/08/23/opinion/the-national-security-agencys-domestic-spying-program.html?_r=2

If anyone is curious as to why the mainstream media has, for the most part, refused to ask any tough questions about post-9/11 surveillance initiatives, this article will shine some light on the matter.

DREW PETERSON CASE: WILL THE GUILTY VERDICT STAND?

SEPTEMBER 9, 2012 AT 4:23 PM | FILED UNDER TRUE CRIME

The saga of a suburban Illinois police sergeant turned bad came-to-an-end last week with the conviction of Drew Peterson—a man Will County prosecutors alleged murdered his third wife of almost 11-years, Kathleen Savio.

Or did it?

Prosecutors say Peterson's life began to unravel in 2003. Just eight days after his divorce from Savio, Peterson, 49, married 19-year-old Stacy Coles. In the interim, payments to Savio, as the result of their divorce, began crimping Drew Peterson's lifestyle.

On March 1, 2004, Peterson returned his sons to Savio's home after a visitation. A series of bizarre events allegedly transpired that should have led any seasoned homicide investigator to believe something was awry.

After pounding on Savio's door without a response, Peterson—a police officer who has likely entered several homes without a warrant under the doctrine of exigent circumstances—decided to contact a neighbor to request the services of a locksmith. In situations like this, police officers generally do one of two things: they either force entry to check the welfare of the person inside or call the police. Seeing how Savio was Peterson's ex-wife, most off-duty officers would have called the local police department to avoid allegations of impropriety.

Peterson, however, did neither.

Then, after the locksmith opened the door to Savio's residence, Peterson—an experienced police officer trained in room clearing—let the neighbor enter first.

The neighbor, a woman, found Kathleen Savio's body inside a dry bathtub. Her hair was soaked in blood. Since Peterson was a member of the local police department, the Illinois State Police conducted the death investigation.

It is important to remember that Savio's life tragically ended in Will County, Illinois—a jurisdiction synonymous with the acronym SNAFU.

In October 2010, Will County authorities arrested Brian Dorian, a small town Illinois police officer, for the so-called honeybee shootings. The Will County State's Attorney—the equivalent of a Wisconsin district attorney—later charged Dorian with first-degree murder based solely on circumstantial evidence. After twisting in the wind for several weeks, forensic investigators later learned that Dorian was logged-on to his computer at the time one of the shootings went down. As such, the Will County State's Attorney abruptly dropped the murder charges against Dorian.

Two months later, a customer struggled with an armed gunman at an Orland Park, Illinois tanning salon. After disarming the perpetrator, the patron shot-and-killed the would-be robber, whose description matched that of the honeybee shooter. Ballistics later confirmed that the firearm recovered from the tanning salon was the same one used in the honeybee shootings.

As was the case with the arrest of Brian Dorian, authorities in Will County—an apparent 21st century backwater—dropped the ball in the Savio death investigation as well.

Patrick O'Neil, the Will County Coroner at the time of Savio's death, was a third-generation family member to hold the elected position, which required little medical experience. At the time, detectives in Will County, not the coroner, ascertained if an autopsy was required.

O'Neil took Savio's flimsy four-page autopsy to a coroner's jury—a body comprised of six lay people selected, randomly, from the community. The coroner's presentation lasted just 45 minutes, at which time the jury concluded that Savio's death was an accident. Making matters worse, one of the jurors was an off-duty police officer, who told other members of the panel that he knew Drew Peterson to be a caring person.

Things changed on October 29, 2007, when Stacy Peterson—Drew's fourth wife—went missing. As of this writing, her whereabouts—more likely, the location of her body—are yet unknown. The sensationalism behind the disappearance—Drew Peterson's law enforcement background and the smell of a potential cover-up—caused Stacy's case to hit the national news networks.

As investigators sought to exhume Kathleen Savio's body for a second opinion, Fox News dispatched former LAPD Detective Mark Fuhrman to Will County to seek additional information. Fuhrman did something that, up until that point, the Illinois State Police had not: he reached into Drew Peterson's background and interviewed his ex-wives.

Peterson's second wife, Victoria, told Fuhrman that Drew attended a locksmith school and typically carried a professional locksmith's case with him. Detective's theorized that this was why Peterson—a former forensic investigator—called for a locksmith to enter Savio's residence. If Peterson had picked-the-lock to Savio's residence, an examination of the mechanism by the crime lab would prove little.

Two steps ahead of Illinois investigators, Fuhrman also contacted Stacy Peterson's minister. After convincing the member of the clergy that Stacy was likely dead, the man told Fuhrman that the night before Savio's body was discovered, Stacy awoke to find Drew Peterson in the downstairs laundry room stuffing women's clothing into the washer. According to the minister, Drew told Stacy, 'You know where I've been. I was taking care of the problem. It'll be the perfect crime.'

Knowing what occurred to Savio, Stacy likely lied to investigators by explaining that Drew Peterson was home the night Kathleen Savio died. Investigators theorize that Peterson might have gotten wind that Stacy had provided details of Savio's death to the minister.

On its face, of course, the evidence points strongly to Drew Peterson's guilt, especially the details provided by Stacy's minister.

One major hurdle for the prosecution was that Stacy Peterson—whereabouts unknown—was unavailable to testify. Moreover, according to the rules of evidence, as well as the Sixth Amendment's confrontation clause, criminal defendants have an absolute right "...to be confronted with the witnesses against him." This meant that the statements of the minister, and possibly other witnesses, would likely be ruled inadmissible at trial.

In 2004, the U.S. Supreme Court, in Crawford v. Washington, 541 U.S. 36 (2004), noted, "Where testimonial evidence is at issue, however, the Sixth Amendment demands what the common law required: unavailability and a prior opportunity for cross-examination...," which means if a witness is unavailable for cross examination at a criminal trial, their statements are hearsay and inadmissible.

Since Justice Antonin Scalia, one of the court's conservative members, authored the Crawford decision, and the ideological make-up of the U.S. Supreme Court remains static, any lawmaker, attorney or politician, swearing an oath to uphold and defend the Constitution should recognize the Crawford decision as the rule of the land.

Apparently, the rule of the land means little to lawmakers or judges in Illinois, where two of that state's former governors currently reside in federal prisons.

In a kneejerk response to the Drew Peterson case, Illinois passed a law that permits hearsay in criminal trials when a witness is unavailable to testify due to an unusual circumstance. Some in the media openly refer to this new provision as 'Drew's law.' The problem is 'Drew's law' flies in the face of the Sixth Amendment and the U.S. Supreme Court's ruling in Crawford v. Washington. Worse yet, members of the judicial system in Illinois believe that 'Drew's law' trumps the Bill of Rights.

Speaking with the media, the jurors who convicted Drew Peterson of murdering Kathleen Savio openly admit it was the hearsay evidence that provided the proof beyond a reasonable doubt to convict.

Because Illinois lawmakers apparently believe that the will of their little fiefdom takes precedent over the Sixth Amendment of the Bill of Rights and a ruling of the U.S. Supreme Court, the Drew Peterson case will linger on appeal for years. Moreover, I predict—barring some type of statement made to a jailhouse snitch while Peterson is behind bars—that this conviction will get overturned. As a result, the taxpayers of Illinois will have to deal with yet another one of their political system's debacles instead of requiring their investigators, lawmakers, and prosecutors, to take the time and get it right. After all, there is no statute of limitations for homicide.

U.S. REP. JIM SENSENBRENNER SUPPORTS LANDMARK PRIVACY BILL

SEPTEMBER 15, 2012 AT 1:57 PM | FILED UNDER CITIZEN TALK

Yesterday, I heard from a person who visits the Spingola Files regarding bill H.R. 2168, the Geolocatonial Privacy Surveillance Act (GPS Act). After learning about this proposed legislation from SF's September 1 post, she contacted Congressman F. James Sensenbrenner to urge the long-time lawmaker to support this important piece of legislation.

In response, Rep. Sensenbrenner replied that he is a supporter of H.R. 2168.

"The law has not kept pace with the assortment of new communication devices and other technologies that are now widely available in today's marketplace," Rep. Sensenbrenner wrote. "As GPS technology has become cheaper, more widely available, and used more frequently in our everyday lives, the legal authorities and restrictions that, are, or should be, in place to govern when such information about another person is accessed and used have become less than clear."

In this letter, Rep. Sensenbrenner also notes that he is a co-sponsor of H.R. 2168 because "H.R. 2168 balances Americans' privacy protections with the legitimate needs of law enforcement, and maintains emergency exceptions."

It is important to note that the GPS Act not only provides protections from the government, but also from private entities.

With drones and nano-drones set to fly and government entities sharing Americans' biometric information, it is important that congress passes laws that keep pace with the introduction of intrusive new technologies.

So get on the horn and give your congressional representatives and U.S. senators a call.

ASK THE COP ON THE BEAT: JOE BIDEN KNOWS BETTER

OCTOBER 14, 2012 AT 7:54 PM | FILED UNDER BATTLEGROUND WISCONSIN

Since the terror attacks of September 11, 2001, federal grants—provided primarily by the U.S. Department of Homeland Security—have gradually incorporated local law enforcement into the national security apparatus. Whether it is a Joint Terrorism Task Force, comprised of federal, state and local officers or the creation of 77 intelligence 'fusion' centers, much of what is fed into the super computers of our nation's intelligence agencies emanates locally.

The trend of having first responders gather data has become so prevalent that criminal justice programs at southeastern Wisconsin technical colleges now offer courses on terrorism and homeland security, which is why some of the comments of Vice President Joe Biden, made during the October 11 Vice Presidential debate, are off-base.

Either Biden just doesn't get it—something I do not personally believe—or he is minimizing the impact of the Iranian nuclear threat.

First, Biden stated that economic sanctions are crippling Iran. Actually, the Iranian mullahs are doing just fine, although the Iranian people might be suffering.

Didn't the Bush Administration try the same strategy with North Korea? Attempts to cajole the Chinese into pressuring North Korean dictator Kim Jong-Il to give up his nuclear weapons program failed miserably. While sanctions did cause the North Korean people to starve, the dictator and his family lived large. Nonetheless, by the end of Bush's second term, North Korea had the ability to deliver a nuclear device. Just this week, the North Koreans claimed to have a delivery system capable of striking the continental United States.

But it is Biden's remark that while the Iranian regime has weapons grade uranium it lacks the ability to deliver a nuclear device that is disingenuous.

Unlike North Korea, the Iranian mullahs are religious extremists. Like other supporters of Jihad, or Islamic holy war, they view the eradication of the infidels, even if it is ultimately suicidal, as something which will be rewarded by Allah in the afterlife. By stringing together a regional terrorist network—the Red Army in Japan, the Secret Army in Armenia, and Hezbollah in Beirut—the

Iranians have the ability to deliver a small nuclear device by through the use of a suicide bomber, an artillery shell or, if need be, in a suitcase.

Furthermore, if Saddam Hussein could strike Israel from Iraq with Scud missiles in 1991, what makes Joe Biden believe the Iranians do not have the ability to hit the Jewish state 21-years later?

After 9/11, the federal government spent a fortune to provide some local police departments, like the NYPD, and agencies that patrol interstate highways, the ability to detect nuclear material. Some of these instruments are so sensitive that Americans who have received radiation treatment for cancer have been stopped and questioned by law enforcement.

Obviously, the reason DHS has funded the purchases of such devices is to detect a portable nuclear device, which leads one to wonder why Biden is babbling about Iranian delivery systems.

More troubling is Biden's belief that the same intelligence agencies that allegedly left the administration out of the loop about the possibility of an attack on the U.S. consulate in Libya can predict, with pinpoint accuracy, when Iran can deliver a nuclear warhead. Apparently, Biden naïvely believes that the American surveillance state—created with billions of federal dollars borrowed from aboard—will live-up to its billing. Based on a handful of failed terrorist attacks, I am skeptical.

In 2009, Muslim convert Abdulhakim Mujahid Muhammad opened fire on a military recruiting office in Little Rock. He brazenly told investigators that his goal was to kill as many members of the armed forces as possible.

A few months later, Umar Farouk Abdulmutallab failed to detonate plastic explosives stored in his underwear during a flight from Europe to Detroit. The intelligence community had information regarding Abdulmutallab's relationship to Islamic extremists in Yeman, but, when authorities misspelt his name by one letter, the government's software failed to identify him as a potential threat.

In 2010, 30-year-old Faisal Shahzad, a Pakistani-born resident of Connecticut, drove an SUV containing explosives to New York City's Time Square. The hundreds of surveillance cameras and hidden chemical sensors failed to detect the device. Fortunately, two street vendors, who observed smoke coming from the vehicle, flagged-down an NYPD officer.

From these bungled attempts, it is easy to image a scenario where the Iranian's might make a small nuclear device available to a terrorist to plant in a subway station, a crowded high school, or a shopping mall. In the aftermath, it would be difficult to link the device to the mullahs, especially if the person who delivered the instrument perishes in the attack.

The good news is federal, state, and local law enforcement understand the potential for such an attack, even if Joe Biden is willing to smile, grimace, and laugh away the seriousness of the Iranian nuclear threat to score cheap political points.

POLICE BLOTTER: GANGSTERS, SHOOTINGS, AND DEFECTIVE CHINESE PRODUCTS

OCTOBER 15, 2012 AT 2:25 PM | FILED UNDER TRUE CRIME

In 1999, the American Film Festival ranked James Cagney as eighth on the list of the "50 Greatest American Screen Legends." One of the actor's famous roles occurred in The Public Enemy, a movie released during the height of prohibition that chronicled a young gangster's rise to power through booze running and violence.

Twenty-six-years after Cagney's passing, a namesake burst onto the scene Sunday after operating his mother's car absent her consent. Authorities in La Crosse County allege that 17-year-old Minnesota native James D. Cagney led police on a chase with speeds approaching 100 miles per hour.

The younger Cagney soon learned that, unlike those car chases from the gangster era, the police are now armed with stop sticks—devices that puncture a vehicle's tires.

Sources on the scene—tongue-in-cheek—overheard a deputy tell the handcuffed Cagney, "You're the guy, see. You're the guy whose attorney's fee are killing your mother."

Could it be naming a child after an actor made famous for portraying gangsters might be an example of labeling theory gone awry?

CHICAGOLAND WORSE THAN THE WILD, WILD WEST

During the debate that led to the passage of Wisconsin's concealed carry law, opponents of the bill argued that the new legislation would turn the state into the wild, Wild West. Predictably, a year after the law's implementation, few, if any, reports of those holding permits abusing their right to carry have materialized.

Yet just 100 miles to the south of Spingola Files' HQ, the city of Chicago is experiencing a major escalation in gun violence.

This past weekend, the sound of gunfire on Chicago's south side resulted in five more homicides and another 25 people wounded.

But wait a minute; I thought Illinois had some of the toughest anti-gun laws in the nation. As of this writing, Illinois is the only state in the union that strictly prohibits concealed carry for members of the general public. In order to purchase a firearm or ammo in the Land of Lincoln, buyers need a special ID that links purchases to the new owners.

Illinois is proof positive that gun control laws simply disarm the innocent with disastrous consequences.

TAKE YOUR MEDICAL PRIVACY AND 'STICK IT'

Signed by President Clinton in 1996, HIPAA—the Health Insurance Portability and Accountability Act—was created, in part, to secure the "protected health information" of Americans. The law includes medical services providers, such as hospitals, doctors, clinics, and ambulance companies.

However, HIPAA did little to safeguard an unnamed Mayville, Wisconsin woman. A small newspaper article, making the rounds on Facebook, notes that this woman called for emergency assistance when a sex toy she used broke-off and lodged in her anus. The article notes that the woman complained of stomach pain, was conveyed to a nearby hospital, where the sex toy was removed.

Some might argue that, since the woman was unnamed, her privacy was not violated. Mayville, however, is a relatively small town, where, I am quite sure; those treated for sex toy anal blockages are few and far between. Cleary, the entity that released this information should be called on the carpet. What occurred, even if it results in a good chuckle, was not a crime. Why a newspaper would find it newsworthy lies in its sensational value.

Remember this incident the next time you hear an advocate of the big brother, American surveillance state say, 'You have nothing to worry about if you have nothing to hide.' Privacy equates to the right of an individual to conceal and/or shield their information from the public domain.

THE LIBRARY DETECTIVE

OCTOBER 8, 2009 AT 2:25 PM | FILED UNDER CITIZEN TALK

Stop by any police district during the day shift. It won't take long before a veteran officer blurts out a remark about 'these young coppers nowadays.' The City of Milwaukee established its police force in 1855, four full generations before I was born. By 1875, I would be willing to bet, some crusty constable at day shift roll call probably scoffed about 'these young coppers nowadays.'

In reality, however, each generation of men and women in blue continues to improve. Today's younger officers are substantially more educated than the crew of the day shift at District 5, where I was assigned as a rookie officer in the late 1970s. Each generation of law enforcement improves by coupling new technologies and new techniques with the experiences gleaned from their predecessors.

As generations of detectives pass along, some interesting cases collect dust, and over time, slowly fade from memory. An old episode of the television series Homicide: Life on the Street, entitled Finnegan's Wake, chronicled the story of a young girl murdered in the 1930s. The case investigator, who had long since died, had passed the file to his younger colleague, Detective Tommy Finnegan, who doggedly pursued all leads but never solved the crime. Believing that the killer likely died of old age, Finnegan took the file home when he retired in the 1970s. When a firearm used in the 60 year-old homicide turned-up in a nearby lake, the current generation of Baltimore homicide detectives located their elderly predecessor, who had the reports stashed in his basement.

During my travels, I haven't had the good fortune to speak with a retired homicide detective a generation or two removed from the job. Then last fall, I reviewed The Library Detective -- an essay written by a local high school senior in support of her application to a prestigious private college. During a visit to the Milwaukee Public Library, this young woman stumbled upon the book Strange People, published in 1961 by Frank Edwards. Inside she located The Case of the Psychic Detective; a story based on the predictions of Arthur Price Roberts, a local Milwaukee man with "strange talents."

On October 18, 1935, the 69 year-old Roberts offered this eerie warning to officials from the Milwaukee Police Department (MPD): "Going to be lots of bombings -- dynamitings! I see two blanks blown up and perhaps city hall. Going to blow up police stations. Then there's going to be a big blow-up south of the river and then it'll be over."

Roberts apparently had some creditability, as the MPD's Detective English immediately contacted his supervisors. The department beefed up patrols, but, just six days later, the bombings began. The village hall in the "small, gold coast suburb" of Shorewood became the first target. Then, on October 27, two bombs exploded outside Milwaukee banks. The culprits later detonated several sticks of dynamite on the doorsteps of two Milwaukee police precincts.

Stunned by the accuracy of these predictions, Detective English rushed to find the aging psychic. Roberts provided this final caveat: "On Sunday, November 4th, there'll be a big one south of the Menomonee [River], and that'll be all."

English quickly contacted the department's brass. Officers soon flooded the "Menomonee District" with orders to shoot first and ask questions later. Then, on the afternoon of November 4, a large blast ripped through Milwaukee's south side, the force of which was felt eight miles from its epicenter. Investigators found the body parts of 21 year-old Idzi Rutkowski and 19 year-old Paul Chovonee spread over several blocks after the 50-pound bomb they constructed unexpectedly detonated.

Curious for more details, the high school senior searched the library's newspaper microfiche.

"Federal agents, deputy sheriffs, and all available members of the police force," said an article in the October 28, 1935 edition of the Milwaukee Journal, "joined Monday in a search for the gang of dynamiters…"

In some instances, unfortunately, law enforcement is its own worst enemy. On November 2, 1935, the Milwaukee Sentinel ran the story Path from Crime to Crime Cleared with Siren, suggesting the bombers procured a police cruiser from the parking lot of a suburban police station to escape detection.

The big news came on November 4. Tragically, the blast also killed nine-year-old neighbor Patricia Mynarek, whose bedroom rested "only a few feet adjacent to the decimated garage" occupied by the bomb makers. The Milwaukee Sentinel quickly identified Rutkowski as a leader of a shadowy south side street gang.

The day after the blast, the Milwaukee Journal published a photograph showing scores of well-dressed men with brimmed hats standing three deep on the sidewalk. "Thousands of curious Milwaukee people," the caption reads, "continued Monday to visit the 2100 block of W. Mitchell Street, where a terrific dynamite blast Sunday afternoon wrote the fatal end to the depredations of Idzi Rutkowski, youthful bomber."

Over the course of time, some things never change. Seventy-four years later, south side gang violence is still in the news, and curious gawkers continue to mill around crime scenes. But unlike the detectives from Homicide: Life on the Street, I never had an opportunity to compare death investigation notes with a throw back like Tommy Finnegan or the MPD's Detective English, even though a high school senior's essay made me wish I had.

Made in the USA
Monee, IL
28 November 2021